POKER'S STRANGEST HANDS

Graham Sharpe

**ROBSON
BOOKS**

First published in the United Kingdom in 2007 by
Robson Books
151 Freston Road
London
W10 6TH

An imprint of Anova Books Company Ltd

ISBN 1 86105 956 6

10 9 8 7 6 5 4 3 2 1

Typeset by SX Composing DTP, Rayleigh, Essex
Printed and bound by Creative Print & Design, Ebbw Vale, Wales

This book can be ordered direct from the publisher.
Contact the marketing department, but try your bookshop first.

www.anovabooks.com

POKER'S STRANGEST HANDS

Other titles in this series:

Contents

To all the boys I used to play brag and poker with in the late sixties, who gave me a brief inkling of what it must be like to be a poker pro. That's the nearest I'll ever get.

About the Author

Graham Sharpe is Media Relations Director for bookmakers William Hill and a prolific author who has written over twenty books with a gambling theme. He knows the game of poker like the back of his hand, having spent a couple of months making a living at the card tables in an earlier phase of his working life.

INTRODUCTION

No one knows for sure how the game of poker came by its name.

It almost certainly derives from a variety of similarly styled card games, such as the Persian 'As Nas', which was played with five cards dealt to two players from a twenty-card deck, containing all 'honour' cards – lion, king, lady, soldier and dancing girl. It also featured pairs, triplets, straights, flushes and bluffs.

Poker historian David Parlett has rubbished the 'As Nas' theory, explaining, 'The problem with this theory is that it is based on no more than a strong resemblance and suffers from a total lack of contemporary evidence, since the earliest descriptions of As Nas do not occur until the 1890s.'

The British three-card game, brag, has many similarities, and in the 1882 book *Poker: How To Play It*, by 'One of its Victims', it is stated, 'it would appear that poker is an immediate development from this latter game'. Another poker researcher, Jeffrey Burton, supports this viewpoint, declaring that what emerged when the two games were brought together 'could equally well have been dubbed five-card brag'.

But poker also shares similarities with Italy's fifteenth-century game Il Frusso, which developed into Prim(i)era or Premiere, or La Prime; France's Gilet; and Spain's Mus while Germany's Pochspiel contained an element of bluffing.

Poker: How To Play It also makes a case for poker to derive from 'Gleek, which was played in England more than three

1

hundred years ago', and another ancient game, 'Pot and Paire'. The book also cites evidence from Ben Jonson's 1596 comedy *Every Man in His Humour*, which contains the phrase 'Here's a trick vied and revied'. A note to the 1816 edition of the comedy explains, 'To vie was to hazard, to put down a certain sum upon a hand of cards. To revie was to cover it with a larger sum, on which the challenged became the challenger, and was to be revied in his turn with a perpetual increase of stake.' The author of *Poker: How To Play It* used this as evidence that, 'long years before the game of Poker reached its present development, its principles were known in this country, and England must be credited with the honour of being the home of its origin'. He went on to envisage the Pilgrim Fathers exporting the game to America, picturing how 'the sweet simplicity of Gleek gradually blossomed out into the fierce and seductive Poker'.

Poker writer Dale Armstrong admitted in his 1977 work *Win at Gin & Poker*, 'Modern poker climbed up through a long line of European and British card games, changing here and cross-breeding there until finally it crystallized into Straight Poker, the basic principles of which govern all Poker games.'

But the leading contender for the source of poker's nomenclature is the French game Poque (pronounced po-kay), apparently introduced to the States by one of the eighteenth-century founders of New Orleans, Jean Baptiste le Moyne. Poque saw three cards dealt to two or three players from a 32-card – all numbered cards – deck.

Gambling expert John Scarne notes, 'I have even heard it argued that Poker derives from the Hindu "pukka" ', but goes on to outline his support for it deriving from underworld slang for a pocketbook or wallet: a poke.

Some claim that the German game Poche or Pochspeil may have been the source of the name – with the word 'poche' once having described an imaginary, bizarre, hobgoblin-like creature. Apparently, the Dutch version of 'pochen' means to act boastfully – which would be appropriate.

Notice that a combination of As Nas and Poque would utilise 52 cards. And both games were popular by the year 1800 in New Orleans. 'They came into the city's life via European sailors,' posited 1950s gambling expert, Jerry D Lewis, 'but it was a group of unknown Americans who did the vital laboratory work of combining the two games.'

From New Orleans the fledgling game spread via the Mississippi steamboats upriver and thence to all points of the compass. 'It caught on as the great American game because it reflected the distinctive traits of the men who played it,' wrote expert Henry Chafetz. Writer Andy Bellin believes that the 'distinctive traits' were not necessarily honourable: 'the fact of the matter is, poker was created by card cheats,' he avowed in *Poker Nation*, adding, 'the inventors were a far cry from the hard-working European ancestors upon whose broken backs this country was built. Poker was conjured out of the smoke-filled air of the saloons of the South by drunks, thieves and gunfighters.'

Scarne believed that the first written reference to poker was made by Jonathan H Green, who, in 1834 or 1843, depending on which source you accept, in a book called *An Exposure of the Arts and Miseries of Gambling*, gave the rules for what he described as a 'cheating game' being played on the steamboats, stating that it was the first time the rules had been published. 'In my opinion,' declared Scarne, 'Poker, like Three-Card Monte, was developed by the card-sharps.'

In the early days the game boasted an almost infinite number of variations – in Toledo, Ohio, they devised a game called Jack Pots in which each player would ante before the deal and in which the first bettor must hold a pair of Jacks at least. Other early variations included Whiskey Poker and Spit in the Ocean. Not all were welcomed by serious players.

In 1860 the A Dougherty Playing Card Company came up with a likely wheeze – they introduced into their packs an extra card, depicting a Court Jester in cap and bells – the Joker. The ability thus afforded to allow the Joker to act as a 'wild' card did not receive universal acclaim.

By 1879 writer John Blackbridge was demanding, 'The time has arrived when all additions to the present standard combinations in draw poker must be worthless, the game already being complete. Neither Jack-Pots, nor any other variation of pure poker should be tolerated by any tradition-loving, decent-minded player.'

Blackridge made a further sage observation, whose truth is evident to this day: 'Poor players usually increase their bets when losing, on the principle that bad play and bad luck united will win. A slight degree of intoxication aids to perfect this intellectual deduction.'

The United States Playing Card Company published a book of poker rules in 1889, and eight years later R F Foster wrote *Hoyle's Encyclopaedia of Indoor Games*, which included poker, thus perpetrating the belief among some that Edmund Hoyle himself, the noted English barrister who had indeed codified the rules of many games, pastimes and sports of his day, was also responsible for doing so to poker. Those who dispute this are on pretty strong ground, as Hoyle died in 1769.

Despite being the home of playing cards, invented there in around AD 975, China did not discover poker until the 1920s, when an American, Carl Crow, editor of a Shanghai newspaper, printed 10,000 copies of a rule book for the traditional, five-card version of the game. This went on to sell over one million copies including, it was said, one to a monastery in Tibet.

The game also caught on in Siam, author Gordon Sinclair reporting, 'Some dentists in Bangkok specialise in poker teeth. Holes in the shape of a heart, spade, club or diamond are drilled in sound front teeth, and filled with green, red, black or light blue cement.'

By 1934 a variation of the game called 'Jackpots – Sevens Wild' was unveiled in the 21 July edition of *Literary Digest*. There were many others: Whiskey Poker, Rum Poker, Gin Poker – are you spotting a theme here?

Phrases deriving from poker have passed into common parlance over the years – for example 'blue chip', signifying top quality, came from the fact that the highest value chips when playing poker were customarily of that colour. The first chips were made of materials like bone, ivory and mother-of-pearl – all materials which, observed poker writer Phil Gordon, 'would nowadays lead animal activists to set your house on fire'. Eventually, though, clay and plastic became the materials of choice.

It is also worth keeping an eye out for unusual chips you may come across. An Ohio man bought one from the defunct Hacienda Casino in a local market and then put it up for sale on eBay – it turned out to be one of a kind, and made $15,000.

POKER'S FIRST HISTORIAN

USA, 1808

Jonathan H Green was born in 1808. He grew up to serve in the 35th Indiana, Company F, and became both an observer of and participant in the world of gambling to such an extent that by the time he reached his eightieth birthday and entered the Soldiers' Home at Dayton, Ohio, to see out his remaining days, he was described as 'a reformed gambler'.

In the intervening years he had made an indelible mark on the world of poker by writing a sequence of books that would act as a history of the early days of the game.

Green makes reference in his books to poker games taking place as early as 1834 and gives details of a game that took place in 1837 on a steamer called *Smelter*, running between Cincinnati and Galena, in which a gambler called John Howard spoke of 'full-deck poker' as being different to the more frequently played and widely known twenty-card poker.

Green wrote of the latter game, 'It would seem to be a variation of the game of Brag, being similar in many particulars, such as making pairs, passing, becoming eldest hand. It is usually played with twenty cards – ace, king, queen, jack, ten of each suit – and by two, three or four persons, each having five cards.'

THE FIRST CHEAT MAKES A GREEN
SPECTACLE OF HIMSELF

LOUISVILLE, 1829

Joe Cowell, a touring actor from England, found himself on board a steamboat chugging along from Louisville en route to Kentucky in December 1829. Cowell observed a game taking place that he recognised as a derivative of the popular gambling game, brag, going by the name of poker.

His account of one hand in the game he watched is possibly the earliest report of skulduggery in a poker game.

Cowell records that on what was a foggy night, the boat ran aground, causing most of the travellers to dash around to see what had happened. He noted one man, wearing distinctive green spectacles and a diamond 'stickpin', who had remained calmly seated, shuffling his pack of cards, and who then got the game under way once more.

'It was his turn to deal and when he ended, he did not lift his cards, but sat watching quietly the countenances of the others. The man on his left had bet ten dollars.' One by one the players, including a young lawyer new to the game, matched the ten dollars, before one player raised a massive $500.

'Green Spectacles' called the $500 before taking up his hand in anticipation. Then, 'he paused for a moment in disappointed astonishment, and sighed, "I pass," and threw his cards upon the table'. The left-hand man then bet 'that $500 and $1000 better!'

What had actually happened, it was by now obvious to 'Green Spectacles', was that his intention to deal himself a pre-ordained winning hand had resulted in the hand going to another player, leaving him with a guaranteed loser in his own hand.

'The young lawyer,' continued Cowell, '. . . had had time to calculate the power of his hand – four kings with an ace – it could not be beat! But still he hesitated at the impossibility, as if he thought it could – looked at the money staked and then put his wallet on the table and called.'

One of his two opponents left had four queens with an ace; the other, four jacks and an ace.

'Green Spectacles', noted Cowell, had discarded a hand of four tens with an ace. He added, deadpan, 'In that pursuit, as in all others, even among the players, some black-sheep and black-legs will creep in, as in the present instance.'

Yes, and green specs, too.

KNIFE ONE, BOWIE

LOUISVILLE, 1832

Not only did James Bowie secure immortality by inventing the eponymous knife, he also became a kind of avenging angel on behalf of the innocent gamblers who were preyed upon by unscrupulous gangs of card sharps who would lure them unsuspectingly into crooked poker games taking place on the riverboats of the time.

In 1832, Bowie was apparently on board the steamer *New Orleans*, as was a young businessman who had been on honeymoon with his wife, mixing business with pleasure in New York, where he had collected $50,000 on behalf of merchants and planters to take back with him to Natchez.

'This young gentleman, who fancied himself as a card player and a man of the world,' according to chronicler of the Mississippi gambling scene Herbert Asbury, writing in the early 1900s, became the target of 'a syndicate of gamblers formed to despoil him'. This group were so thorough in their preparations they had sent one of their number to make the newlywed's acquaintance in New York.

'When the young gentleman took a boat at Pittsburgh the sharper was on board, and so were two "Louisiana planters", who made themselves very agreeable,' recorded Asbury. A poker game was suggested and the young honeymooner was soon several hundred dollars up. They were getting on so well that it seemed only natural that the 'planters' and the sharper should accompany them on the *New Orleans*.

Well, no sooner had they departed from Louisville than the

9

man was invited to sit down again for a few hands of poker, and with the gloves off he had soon lost – well, been relieved of – $45,000, and was becoming desperate as he watched his fortune disappear.

At the Vicksburg stop James Bowie boarded, 'wearing a black, broad-brimmed slouch hat and black broad-cloth clothing of clerical cut, and became an interested spectator of the game, which he saw immediately was crooked'.

The young man lost more and more, until finally he saw his last dollar disappear. In a fit of remorse he ran to the boat's rail intending to throw himself overboard.

Bowie helped the young man's new bride restrain him and took him back to their cabin before returning to the bar, where he 'casually displayed a bulging wallet and asked for change for a hundred dollar bill. One of the gamblers, who were opening wine to celebrate the success of their coup, obliged, and after a few moments of conversation suggested a card game, to which Bowie agreed.

On the first few hands Bowie won, and then the sharpers began to forge ahead. At length one of the 'planters' dealt Bowie a hand which any Poker player would bet as long as he could see, and which Bowie recognised as being intended for the big cleanup.

The 'planters' dropped out after a few bets, but Bowie and the 'merchant' continued to raise each other until $70,000 was piled on the table between them. Finally, Bowie saw what he had been watching for – the gambler's hand flicking quickly into his sleeve. Like lightning Bowie seized the sharper's wrist, at the same time drawing from his shirt-bosom a wicked-looking knife.

'Show your hand,' he commanded. 'If it contains more than five cards I shall kill you!'

The gambler attempted to break loose, but Bowie twisted his wrist and his cards fell to the table – four aces, a queen and a jack.

'I shall take the pot,' said Bowie, 'with a legitimate Poker hand, four kings and a ten.'

'Who the devil are you anyway?' cried the discomfited gambler. 'I,' said the famous duellist, 'am James Bowie!'

A contemporary report of the incident records: 'The voice was like velvet, but it cut like steel into the hearts of the chief gambler's confederates and deterred them from any purpose or impulse they might have had to interfere. They, with the crowd, shrank back from the table, smitten with terror by the name. Bowie softly swept the banknotes into his large slouch hat and lightly clapped it to his head.'

There are two versions of the drama's final act – according to one he let the gambler go on his way with a warning, but in the more dramatic account he was challenged by the gambler to a duel, which resulted in the death of the card sharp.

What *is* agreed upon is that Bowie 'gave the young gentleman of Natchez two-thirds of the contents of the hat and kept the remainder as spoils of war.

'With tears in his eyes the young gentleman swore never to touch another card, and both he and his bride prayed that Heaven might bless their benefactor.'

Oh, well, not all prayers are answered – Bowie died just four years later, along with Davy Crockett, in defence of the Alamo.

MARK MY WORDS

MISSOURI, 1835

Samuel Clemens was born on 30 November 1835 in Hannibal, Missouri. He would become the USA's first major literary talent and also one of its greatest lovers of poker.

The name will not ring a bell with anyone other than the most dedicated of readers, because Clemens, who worked as a riverboat pilot in his early days, would come to public attention under the pseudonym of Mark Twain, a man who would declare, 'I have known clergymen, good men, kind-hearted, liberal, sincere and all that, who did not know the meaning of a "flush". It is enough to make one ashamed of one's species.'

Clemens started writing for the Virginia City Territorial Enterprise under his new name, which derived from a phrase for two fathoms of safe depth, familiar from his riverboat days. Another source suggests the name came from his days in the West where he would buy two drinks at a time and tell the barkeeper to 'mark twain' on his bill.

In 1860, Twain heard from a Mississippi river captain, George Newhouse, the tale – possibly apocryphal – of a 'courageous Jew' who saved a slave girl caught up in a poker dispute between a planter and a knife-wielding gambler by killing the cheater and returning the slave girl to her mistress. In later life he would become a noted defender of Jews from persecution.

His first well-known writing dated from 1865 when he wrote 'The Celebrated Jumping Frog of Calaveras County'.

Twain's gambling interests included steamboat races, which

12

he felt were much more compelling than horse racing, and cock-fighting. In his *Life on the Mississippi* he delved into his knowledge of poker to tell the tale of riverboat card-sharps out to fleece a backwoods farmer, which climaxes with the cheats drawing four kings in the big showdown pot, to which the farmer showed four aces and pulled out a revolver, telling the cheats, 'I'm a professional gambler and I've been laying for you duffers all this voyage.'

Twain himself was a decent draw poker player, having learned the game as a boy. It was said by a contemporary on the *Bohemian* newspaper, C H W Inigo, testifying during an 1865 court case, that Twain 'can play equal to any man. [I] consider myself some at draw poker, but he can discount me every time. He won those sleeve buttons that he has on from me at draw poker.'

Twain weathered a financial storm in his life with the assistance of oil magnate Henry Rogers, with whom he once went on a Caribbean cruise, together with Congressman T B Reed. The cards were brought out for poker and at one point Twain recalled Reed winning 23 pots in succession.

So intent on the game were the men that the ship's captain was ordered not to dock the boat at the intended venues, but to 'sail on and do not interrupt the game'.

Twain wrote of a poker game aboard a steamboat in his 1873 work *The Gilded Age*, which featured a congressman, of whom one character observed, 'Looks like a Washington man; I shouldn't think a representative in Congress would play poker in any way in a public steamboat,' only to be told by another, 'Nonsense, you've got to pass the time. The Delegate knows all the points. I'd bet a hundred dollars he will ante his way right into the United States Senate when his territory comes in. He's got the cheek for it.'

Twain eventually died on 21 April 1910, of heart failure, forever immortalised as the author of *The Adventures of Tom Sawyer* and *The Adventures of Huckleberry Finn*.

FEAT OF CLAY

NASHVILLE, C. 1846

Henry Clay (1777–1852) was a popular politician of his day, known as the 'Great Commoner' and credited along with President Abraham Lincoln with being one of the men who saved the Union.

Clay, who stood unsuccessfully for the presidency on several occasions, was also a very keen poker player. In fact, he has been credited with being one of those who modified brag into poker in the early days of the game. He belonged to an exclusive club in Nashville.

One day a stranger managed to secure an invitation to take part in the game. At the climax of the biggest hand of the evening the stranger showed three aces and made to collect the pot.

Clay asked him to wait before he picked up the money. He went over to the wall where a Bowie knife was hanging up, which he removed and brought back to the table, flipping over his own hand with the point of the knife, to reveal two pairs – tens and . . . aces.

The gambler immediately pushed the pot towards the politician and headed speedily for the exit, having been exposed as a card sharp. As he rushed for safety, Clay raised his arm to throw the knife after the fleeing cheat.

As he did so one of his fellow players shouted, 'Hit him in the ace!'

Clay roared with laughter, causing his arm to jerk and the knife to miss its target by inches as the gambler made it to the door and freedom – dishonoured but alive.

Another story is told of a heads-up poker match between Clay and Senator Daniel Webster, who was three times secretary of state under different presidents.

Webster dealt a hand of draw poker. Clay took one hand; Webster stood pat. The pair were betting and raising, pushing the pot up to over $2,000. The two men eyed one another, as Clay called Webster's final raise.

Webster, convinced he had lost, shamefacedly showed a pair of deuces.

'That beats ace high,' said Clay. 'You win.'

THEY PLAYED FOR HOW LONG?

AUSTIN, TEXAS, 1853

LJ Ludovici, a former World War II squadron leader, wrote a book called *The Itch for Play*, published in 1962, at which point, to judge from the photograph on the inside back cover, he was approximately 109 years old. If that is an accurate estimate then he would have been born round about the time – 15 June 1853 – at which, so he tells us in his book, a certain Major Danielson and another Texan, known as 'Old Man' Morgan, sat down to play poker.

LJ pins the precise start time down to 'eight in the evening', and by dawn the next day 'they had agreed to abolish any limit to the stakes'.

The game, reports Ludovici, 'progressed', and exactly how it progressed I will let our flying ace inform you in his own words.

'It continued week after week, month after month and, as it turned out, year after year. The two men rose only to eat, snatch some sleep, answer nature, or change some part of their property into cash so they could play on.'

Apparently, 'Texans flocked to watch them bent solemnly over their cards' – well, perhaps there wasn't much else to do in Texas in those days.

'The railways were built and reached Austin, hotels sprang up everywhere, the Civil War was fought and reconstruction commenced. These events flowed right over the heads of Major Danielson and 'Old Man' Morgan.'

Yes, I know it sounds pretty unlikely, but LJ looks like a man of his word and I for one am prepared to allow him the benefit

16

of the doubt, so read on:

'In 1870, seventeen years after they first sat down, they were still at it.' Stretching credulity, I accept.

'In 1872 both died at one and the same moment.' Mmm, it does seem that LJ is testing our gullibility ever so slightly.

'In their wills they instructed their sons to carry on where they had left off. Their sons obeyed. After the sons had played for another five years . . .' – hold on, that makes it, er . . . seventeen years, two more, um, five extra – that makes it 1877, by my calculation.

'. . . one was killed by a railway train and the other went off his head. The families became impoverished. Today [i.e. 1962] the cards with which Major Danielson and 'Old Man' Morgan started their family card-marathon are said to lie, soiled, torn, curling at the ends and yellowing in the safe deposit of a bank at Austin.'

See – there it is, all you sceptics who think this could be an ever so slightly apocryphal yarn – all you have to do is get on the Internet and check out all the banks in Austin. One of them will undoubtedly confirm the story – or my name's not L J Ludovici.

Which, of course, it isn't.

HONESTY FAR FROM BEST POLICY

MISSISSIPPI, 1858

Celebrating his fiftieth birthday in 1858, professional gambler John Powell, a poker expert, could claim to have built up a fortune of half a million dollars through his shrewd but honest play.

He was a real rarity – contemporary estimates calculated that of some 2,000 riverboat gamblers operating on the Mississippi waters aboard the flourishing steamboats, just a fraction were honest folk. One writer suggested he knew of just four above-board operators.

Powell had just taken part in a poker game aboard the steamer *Atlantic*, in which he played for three days and nights, running up his share of the $791.50 bar bill among the four players, but winning $50,000. He then became involved in a game with a young English traveller, shortly after his half-century celebrations, winning his entire fortune of $8,000, together with his luggage.

The Englishman, showing typical stiff-upper-lip control, accepted his loss and retired to his cabin for the night.

Next morning he appeared in the dining saloon for breakfast. He shook hands with fellow passengers before shooting himself dead.

Powell was so distraught that he discovered where the young man lived and sent the $8,000 and the luggage back to his family. He also gave up gambling for a year as a form of penance.

Returning to the profession, Powell discovered he had lost the element of ruthlessness from his game and soon began to become a regular loser. Eventually his decline contributed to his death. Said one unimpressed writer, 'He died broke – an example to his colleagues of the dangers of compassion.'

The prevalence of dishonest riverboat gamblers in those almost lawless days was highlighted in a book called *The Gamblers* (Time Life Books, 1978), which explained: 'They preferred to stalk their prey in pairs or in teams of three or half a dozen. Often they boarded the boats at different times or at different towns and pretended not to know each other.'

It went on to describe how, by a combination of dodgy dealing and secret signs – including puffing cigar smoke like 'Indian signals' – they would relieve the unfortunate victim of their cash.

DOUBLE DEALER

DENVER, 1860

Jack O'Neil, a towering New Yorker, moved to Denver where he and his girlfriend Salt Lake Kate opened a card table in the first saloon in town, the Hote (sic) de Dunk.

O'Neil had a run-in at the races with a good-for-nothing member of a gang of gamblers and drinkers known as the Bummers.

O'Neil had called the man, John Rooker, a coward, and talk of revenge was in the air when the pair both sat down to play poker at the Western Saloon on 29 March 1860.

Inevitably, O'Neil and Rooker went toe to toe with each other on the green baize table and eventually they were contesting the biggest pot of the night when O'Neil called Rooker's final bet and the ruffian declared, 'Two pairs of pictures.'

'Three jacks,' called O'Neil, and made to take the money.

'Hold it,' demanded Rooker. 'Both my pairs are kings.'

O'Neil made a lunge for Rooker's arm. 'You did not call right. The money is mine.'

The money was forgotten as the two traded insults and threats. As word of the showdown spread, heavy gambling began on the outcome of the dispute.

O'Neil had gone home to bed after the row, and rose at 10 a.m. He strolled up the town's main thoroughfare and, as he reached the entrance to the Western Saloon, he was blasted with both barrels of a shotgun, fired from a safe distance by the cowardly Rooker, who immediately fled town.

O'Neil was buried the next day in a small graveyard which became known as 'O'Neil's Ranch', a term that would become used to identify graveyards in other towns.

UNFROHOCKED

TEXAS, 1870

Captain William Frohock had emerged from the brutal Battle of Fort Lancaster in late 1867 against a band of Native Americans, with his reputation as an inspirational leader of troops enormously enhanced. However, he found himself facing a court martial, having been accused of being guilty of 'conduct unbecoming an officer' – to wit, an 1868 incident in which he had allegedly indulged in a game of poker against a civilian stagecoach driver.

Apparently, Maine-born Frohock, who had been commissioned in 1861 and served under Ulysses S Grant, had lost a substantial amount of money to the driver, only to renege on the debts, at which point he was confronted by the irate man, who forced him to settle up at the point of a gun.

Frohock was found guilty even though, strictly speaking, the gambling itself was not an illegal act.

Despite a review of the case by superior officers, after which the original verdict was overturned, the distraught Frohock resigned his commission. It was later alleged by the regimental commander, Colonel Edward Hatch, that Frohock had also indulged in gambling and poker playing with his own troops as well as other civilian employees.

To add salt to the wounds, Frohock was said to have 'raffled off his effects among the men of the company and gambled in their presence with these employees' when he had submitted his resignation.

In all probability, Frohock was paying the price for

antagonising his regimental superiors in some way. Whether this may have been related to the fact that he commanded the 58 black troopers of Company K is unknown, but writer Wayne R Austerman, an expert on this period of history, later wrote in *Wild West* magazine, 'If he (Frohock) did gamble with his own troops and government employees under his supervision, he assuredly should have been censured. Even so, the suspicion lingers that there was more to the situation than meets the eye at the distance of 135 years.'

Frohock disappeared into the obscurity of civilian life and died on 10 April 1878.

QUEEN HIGH?

SOMERSET, 1871

Queen Victoria awarded the game of poker an unexpected seal of approval in 1871 (some say '72) when it became obvious that she was, indeed, amused by the game.

General Robert Cumming Schenk (born 1809) had been appointed as US Envoy to Britain by President Grant. Schenk was an inveterate poker player, and while he was a guest at Her Majesty's summer estate in Somerset, he decided to lighten the atmosphere by suggesting a game of poker to some of the assembled male guests.

The game was under way when in walked Queen Victoria, who insisted on sitting in on the game, despite her complete ignorance of its rules. Schenk, as it was later reported, 'under strict orders from President Grant to create no incidents', duly agreed to teach his royal hostess how to play.

'The amount is unrecorded,' says an account of the occasion, 'but Victoria must have been a healthy winner, because she announced immediately after the game that she was delighted with it.'

She was so delighted she requested Schenk to supply her with a written set of rules. Schenk complied and in so doing sparked the very kind of incident Grant had feared.

Delegations descended on the White House demanding his recall, letters were written to newspaper editors in the strongest possible terms condemning him, and he was even burned in effigy.

What could be responsible for such outrage? Was it because

24

he was encouraging the monarch and, by implication, her subjects, to gamble? Partly, maybe, and also partly because poker was very much a male game in those days, not considered suitable for ladies (particularly ladies of breeding), but the real cause of the uproar was a phrase Schenk had included in the written rules he had supplied to the queen and which had been printed for all to see in his pamphlet of 1875, 'Draw Poker'.

'It is a great object to mystify your adversaries up to the call, when hands must be shown. To this end, it is good practice to chaff (or talk nonsense), with a view to misleading your opponents as to the value of your hand.'

Good grief! The fellow was positively encouraging and endorsing bluffing or, as it was then known in the States, the art of 'coffee house'. Poker purists felt this was tantamount to cheating, and an immoral practice.

Schenk survived the storm and remained as envoy for several more years. Although Queen Victoria did not become a professional player, her interest in the game meant it became very much in vogue in court circles, and if she happened to play, she always had at least queen high to gamble on!

Schenk's pamphlet was expanded into book form and was privately printed and published in 1880 – the year of his death.

**Royal interest in poker was rekindled in 2005 when England rugby union player Mike Tindall revealed that he was trying to interest his girlfriend, Princess Anne's daughter Zara Phillips, in the game – 'She has played it a couple of times online,' he revealed.

BANK ON THAT

SAN FRANCISCO, C. 1872

William Ralston was President of the Bank of California – and a keen poker player, for enormous stakes.

In the early 1870s, poker was all the rage in California, with some massive games taking place at the Pacific Club in San Francisco, of which Ralston was a member.

But one particular hand played out there dwarfed all the others and was recorded by an anonymous contemporary account. 'Five of the big fish (a word which would later come to describe poor poker players, but indicated high-rollers at this time) were in the game and they were playing jack pots. (William) Sharon opened, and Ralston and two others stayed.'

Bets of $100 and $200 were thrown in several times, before Ralston began to raise by thousands of dollars. Soon the action was between Sharon and Ralston, with '$150,000 in the pot. Then Sharon met a raise with a $50,000 counter. Ralston studied only a moment and then came back with a raise of $150,000.'

With in excess of $350,000 on the table, Sharon folded his hand and shuffled it back into the deck. Ralston laid down his pair of tens in delight before collecting the pot. Sharon resisted all efforts to persuade him to say what was in his hand until after Ralston's death.

'It was a pair of jacks.'

Another, possibly apocryphal story, from this very era is told in an 1896 book of poker anecdotes by John F B Lillard.

The chief cashier of a bank in Denver arrived for work one

morning to be greeted by three men sitting on the steps of his establishment.

'Want to make a deposit?' he asked them.

'No, I want to negotiate a $5,000 loan,' replied a man holding an envelope.

'What is your collateral?'

The man told him: 'I've been sitting in a poker game across the street and there's $4,000 in the pot. Every cent I have is on the table and I have been given thirty minutes to raise a stake on my hand, which is in this envelope. Just look at it.'

The cashier ripped open the envelope and found inside four kings and an ace – an unbeatable hand at the time.

'We don't lend money on cards,' he said.

As he turned to leave, the bank's president arrived on the scene. When he saw the gambler's cards he immediately grabbed a bag of $20 bills and followed the man back to the game, returning within minutes to toss the original money and an extra handful of bills to the cashier who had turned down the loan request.

'Ever play poker?' he asked.

'No, sir.'

'Thought not. If you did you'd have known what good collateral that hand was. Remember that in future four kings and an ace are always good in this institution for our entire assets, sir – our entire assets.'

POKER'S GREATEST TRAGEDY?

NEW MEXICO, 1873

John Peters was a reformed character. The professional poker player and gambler, wanted for murder in New Orleans, had fallen for a saloon beauty, Ann Masters, on the Barbary Coast, renounced his former profession and whisked his new love away from her own seedy lifestyle.

They set up a straight gambling club, the Casa Rouge, in the small town of Anton-Chicot (now Chico) where, in a symbolic renouncing of his past, he became known as Jean Pierres. The pair lived happily in domestic bliss, and their casino – the only honest one in town – flourished.

In the spring of 1873 a no-good villain, Mike Shaw, came to town, drinking and gambling to excess. Shaw was not above resorting to cheating to assist his chances of winning at poker and had been run out of New York, Chicago, San Francisco, Denver and Santa Fe before ending up in Anton-Chicot.

He was playing poker at the Casa Rouge when he was accused of sneaking a card from the deck. An argument broke out and Pierres, who was in the vicinity inspecting the conduct of the tables, intervened just as Shaw drew a gun, knocking it out of his hand.

Shaw charged at Pierres with a knife. Pierres also pulled a blade in order to protect himself and as they struggled each stabbed the other in the arm. Shaw swore vengeance as he was dragged out of the Casa Rouge.

One morning, Pierres awoke early and dressed carefully, awaking the eight-month pregnant Masters, who had a

28

premonition something was about to happen and cautioned Pierres to stay where he was.

Pierres took his pistol and departed.

That afternoon Pierres and Shaw met up and a gun fight ensued, resulting in Pierres slumping to the ground with a fatal wound, gasping out his last words, 'Thank God, I die dressed like a gentleman.'

Masters arrived on the scene almost unnoticed in the crowd. When she realised what had happened she moved towards Shaw and plunged a stiletto knife into his throat, spitting at him, cursing him and screaming obscenities at him as he died at her feet.

Masters collapsed and was carried back to her room where, later that night, her baby was born, only to die almost immediately. She hovered at death's door herself; when she finally recovered, she sold off the Casa Rouge and left Anton-Chicot for ever.

Pierres and Shaw were buried next to each other in the local cemetery.

SHARP PRACTICE

NEW YORK, 1874

New York City attorney John Blackbridge was a keen poker player who had for some years suspected that cheating in the game was rife but had never had his suspicions confirmed until, in 1874, he received a visitor who proved it conclusively before his very eyes.

Blackbridge was so taken aback that he wrote a book called *Practical Guide-Book*, published in 1880, in which he attempted to alert his readers to the dangers of playing poker against strangers, who were very likely to be 'sharpers' out to take them for all they could get.

'If card-sharpers exist, and they certainly do, because now and then they are detected, under what circumstances shall we find them?' Blackbridge pondered, before answering his own question. 'We shall find them among people of means, playing a game that admits of card manipulation, and that is played for money. The game of poker exactly satisfies these conditions.'

Blackbridge explained that he suspected poker of being plague with sharpers for years, and had his fears confirmed when, in 1874, a man visited his office and showed him how it was done.

The man, about forty, first demonstrated to Blackbridge how he could conceal any two cards he wished in his left hand while dealing. Then how he could deal from the bottom of the pack, along with a slew of other tricks: he dealt him three aces, then four aces, all while Blackbridge watched him closely.

'This man stated to me, and indeed it is very obvious, that a manipulator does not need to manipulate all the time in order to win. He need only do it at critical periods, as for instance when the luck is running against him, or when he has a four flush, or four straight; or two pairs, "aces up".'

The man impressed on Blackbridge the principle that these tricks only needed to be pulled at certain critical times. 'A card sharper must not be over greedy, and must not overdo the business,' he explained.

The moral of Blackbridge's warnings was that players should stick to games of modest stakes – or suffer the consequences. 'No one ever abandons Poker that plays it on small limited stakes. Sharps will not play such a game, and as it never leads to ill results it prospers forever by its own merits, like the simple, healthy and unforced growth of a plant that is nourished by Nature.'

POKER BLOSSOMS

1875–1900

As soon as poker began to spread as a popular gambling game, people wanted to read about it – and authors to write about it.

And by the turn of the nineteenth century there was already a pretty extensive body of work beginning to fill the bookshelves and libraries of the day.

In 1875 the marvellously named Henry T Blossom burst into print with *The Game of Draw Poker, Mathematically Illustrated*.

Also among the earliest of titles were 1880's 142-page *The Complete Poker Player*, written by John Blackbridge, which saw the light of day around the same time as Robert C Schenk's (the man who interested Queen Victoria in the game) 1875 pamphlet 'Draw Poker', and his 1880 expanded book version, *Rules for Playing Poker* (available for purchase at a hefty £887 from a rare book dealer in 2006).

In 1881, Jack Abbott's *Treatise on Jackpot Poker* was published in New Orleans, and just one year later Griffith & Farran in London published *Poker; How To Play It* by the otherwise completely anonymous 'One of its Victims'.

Perhaps ashamed of his association with the game, the real author of a 50-page poker work published in New York in 1883 hid behind the pseudonym in the title of the work: *Talk of Uncle George*.

The thirteen pages of Robert J Gilkie's 1886 offering, 'Experimental Drawing at Poker from Five Thousand Hands', sounds riveting. And the same year also saw E Archer Gray's sixteen-page 'Hints on Poker'.

In 1895 along came what was presumably the first poker book by a woman – although with the author's name given as Alice Howard Cady it isn't completely clear as to her/his sex!

In 1896 F Jarvis Patton put pen to paper for 'How to Win at Draw Poker', published by Dick & Fitzgerald of New York. And in this year the first poker magazine – the monthly *Poker Chips*, 'devoted to stories of the great American game'– made an appearance, surviving between June and November of the year.

Also in 1896 John F B Lillard edited a fascinating compilation of *Poker Stories*, as told by 'statesmen, soldiers, lawyers, commercial travellers, bankers, actors, editors, millionaires, members of the Ananias club and the talent, embracing the most remarkable games 1845–95'.

As the century ended, Eugene Edwards' *Jack Pots*, with anecdotes from 'the great American game' embellished by 'over fifty original pen and ink illustrations', emerged in 1900 from Chicago's Jamieson-Higgins Co, boasting a hefty 342 pages.

CUSTER'S LAST HAND?

LITTLE BIG HORN, 1876

Not only did the US lose one of its greatest generals in June 1876 when Native Americans wiped out George Armstrong Custer and his outnumbered men – it also lost a pair of its keenest poker players.

For both Custer and his younger brother Captain Tom Custer, who was with him on that fateful day, had a history of controversial poker playing behind them.

George's playing had nearly led him into big trouble with the military authorities when, in the late 1860s, he was apparently in the habit of gambling regularly with his subordinate officers in the 7th Cavalry. Worse, he was accused of welching on his poker debts by at least one of those officers. This charge, according to historians, created something of a rift between officers in the unit 'that endured until the Battle of the Little Bighorn', according to authority Wayne R Austerman, even though charges were never actually filed against him.

Brother Tom was perhaps an even more enthusiastic – and somewhat better – poker player. Author Carl Sifakis, calls him 'the best poker player in the 7th Cavalry, an organisation renowned nearly as much for its gambling prowess as for its fighting abilities'.

By all accounts he was something of a reckless player who would wager big stakes and thought nothing of bluffing with abandon in order to bully his opponents out of the game.

His most infamous hand saw him dealt the six, seven and ten of spades. He raised the stakes, hoping to draw more spades.

Table rules were that any card accidentally exposed on the original deal must be taken, but one turned over on the draw would be voided and another dealt in its place.

Custer's first draw card was the eight of spades, much to his delight. The second, as everyone could see when it struck his hand as it was dealt, and turned face up, was the king of spades, which would have completed his flush, as became obvious to all the players as Custer began to swear and curse.

Knowing the rules, though, Custer had to be dealt another card, which he duly accepted with a glare.

As the betting continued, Custer raised aggressively, with the rest of the players assuming he was, as usual, bluffing. Eventually, everyone called and the cards were revealed – Custer's glares turned to grins as he showed a straight flush. The card he had received instead of the king of spades had been the nine of spades.

WHAT'S UP, DOC?

FORT GRIFFIN, 1876

Doc Holliday was born in 1851 in South Carolina. His mother died when he was fifteen of tuberculosis. Shortly afterwards he was involved in an incident in which he killed at least one, possibly more, soldiers and was forced to leave town.

He was sent by his father to study dentistry at college in Baltimore – where he was lured into gambling halls, becoming an expert card player – from where he graduated in 1872. He moved to Georgia to practise but was already showing signs of the tuberculosis that would claim his life.

Doc set off for the dry climate of Texas which, it was thought, might extend his life expectancy. He set up a practice in Dallas, but as his illness worsened he became a professional poker player. In early 1876 he shot a man in a gambling dispute and quit Dallas.

In Jacksboro he killed a soldier at another gambling table and headed to Denver – slaying three more men en route and a couple more when he got there. Two more were dispatched as he headed to Cheyenne, Wyoming.

He met up with 'Big Nose' Kate Elder, the love of his life, and in 1877 met the legendary lawman Wyatt Earp in Fort Griffin. The men hit it off and Wyatt witnessed (and later described) a dramatic event involving Holliday.

Holliday was in a poker game one night and had reason to warn the player on his right, one Ed Bailey, about cheating. But Bailey continued trying to mess around with the discards until Holliday, losing patience, claimed the pot without showing his hand, which, said Earp, 'he had a perfect right to do'.

Bailey went for his gun, but before he could shoot, Holliday whipped out his knife and slashed him across the chest. He slumped across the table, dead.

'Well,' continued Earp:

. . . that broke up the game and pretty soon Doc was sitting cheerfully in the front room of the hotel, guarded while the gamblers clamoured for his blood. Ed Bailey was well liked. Big Nose Kate heard about the trouble and went up to take a look at her Doc. What she saw and heard led her to think that his life wasn't worth ten minutes purchase, and I don't believe it was.

There was a shed at the back of the lot and a horse was stabled in it. She set fire to the shed. The shed blazed up and she hammered at the door, yelling 'Fire!' Everybody rushed out except the marshal and the constables and their prisoner. Kate walked in, threw one of her six-shooters on the marshal and handed the other to Doc Holliday. 'Come on, Doc,' she said with a laugh.

The two of them backed out of the hotel, keeping the officers covered. The pair of them got safely away and rode the four hundred miles to Dodge City.

Continuing to murder the occasional unfortunate and to haul in cash at the poker table, Doc would drink up to four quarts of whiskey a day when his coughing fits were bad.

Now living in Tombstone, Arizona, having arrived there in 1880 on the back of a reported $40,000 poker windfall from his play in the town of Prescott, Doc had become 'the most dangerous man alive,' according to Earp.

In 1881 he fell out with Kate, who in revenge accused him of masterminding a stage robbery.

Doc survived this setback to take part in the gunfight at the OK Corral in January 1882, along with the Earp brothers. He died on 8 November 1887 after his illness forced him to become bedridden for 57 days.

DEAD MAN'S HAND

DEADWOOD GULCH, 1876

Wild Bill Hickok, sometime lawman and gambler, was a long-haired, flamboyant, well-known figure of the day, known by reputation and deed wherever he went.

He rode into the lawless Deadwood Gulch and took up residence, deciding to check out the local poker tables. He fancied himself as something of a skilled player. The truth was, though, as gambling writer Carl Sifakis confirms, 'Hickok was a lousy card player and most of his biographers admit that he lost more money than he won at poker.' It was also said of him, 'It is not improbable that his reputation as a gunfighter won for him many a stake over the poker table which his cards could not win.'

Bill played draw poker, playing fairly as a rule. However, an encounter with a less scrupulous gambler named McDonald had already ensured Bill's place in poker lore.

They had played in Sioux City some years earlier. McDonald beat Bill frequently, and Bill was eventually tipped off that his opponent was almost certainly not playing strictly within the permitted rules.

They sat down again in a no-limit, one-on-one game, drinking as they played. Midnight came and the game was still going strong. Bill had picked up what he thought was a winning hand and was betting accordingly.

Finally, McDonald showed his hand – three jacks.

'I have a full house – three aces and a pair of sixes,' declared Bill, throwing his cards face down on the table.

McDonald lifted them one by one. 'I see only two aces and one six.'

Bill whipped out his six-shooter, saying, 'Here's my other six.' Then he produced a knife – 'And here's my one-spot.'

McDonald knew when he was beaten and conceded the pot.

On 2 August 1876, Bill, who reportedly had a premonition that he would not leave town alive, joined a poker game at the Nuttal and Mann saloon. The three other players were named Carl Mann, Captain William Massie and Charlie Rich. Vitally, and uncharacteristically, he sat in a chair not backed up against a wall.

As he played, a drunken cowboy known as Jack 'Crooked Nose' McCall, with whom Hickok had had a dispute over a 25-cent pot in an earlier hand, entered the saloon and took it into his mind to shoot his 39-year-old victim in the back of the head. Later reports would suggest he was acting at the behest of a gambler called Johnny Varnes, who had lost out in a row with Hickok at the Senate Saloon in Deadwood.

Whatever the motive, Bill slid silently to the floor, still clutching his cards – a pair of aces and a pair of eights. The other card has been variously identified, but most reports suggest a queen.

From that day forward, superstitious gamblers have described a hand boasting a pair of aces and eights as the 'dead man's hand'.

McCall was tried, set free, retried – and hanged.

KING CARNEY'S COMEUPPANCE

DODGE CITY, 1877

Thomas Carney had been Governor of Kansas from 1863 to 1865, but by 1877 he was a wealthy businessman who fancied himself as something of a hustler at the poker tables.

He visited Dodge City, hoping to fleece some wealthy novice players out of a substantial sum by wheedling his way into a big-time game on the pretext of being in town on business.

The local paper, the *Dodge City Times*, had clearly been alerted about Carney and carried a fascinating story about his exploits on the green baize, in which they accused him of intending to 'entice our unsophisticated denizens into the national game of draw poker. The Governor's reputation and dignified bearing soon enabled him to decoy three of our businessmen into a social game,' reported the paper, overlooking the fact that Messrs Norton (Colonel Charles), Robert Gilmore and Charlie Ronan were actually professional gamblers.

'The game proceeded merrily for some time until, under the bracing influence of exhilarating refreshments, the stakes were increased, and the players soon became excitedly interested.'

They were playing with a deck of 53 cards including a joker or wild card, known as a 'cuter', that could be played as an ace and which looked much like the ace of spades to a casual glance.

'At last the Governor held what he supposed to be an invincible hand,' said the *Times*. 'It consisted of four kings and the cuter, which the Governor very reasonably supposed to be the Ace of Spades.'

The stakes mounted rapidly in $100 increments, and 'Governor Carney's eyes glistened with joy as he saw the pile of treasure, which soon would be all his own, loom up before his vision, and he hastened to see the Colonel and add the remainder of his funds, his elegant gold watch and chain.' Norton called him.

It was time for Carney to show his hand, and he gleefully laid down his four kings on the table and prepared to claim his winnings. 'But at that moment a sight met the old Governor's gaze which caused his eyes to dilate with terror, a fearful tremor to seize his frame, and his vitals to almost freeze with horror.' For Colonel Norton now laid down before him four aces.

Carney, 'slowly and reluctantly', relinquished his prize and, 'with a weary, almost painful effort', got up from the table and left the room, muttering to himself, 'I forgot about the cuter.'

The *Dodge City Times* was not content to record Carney's downfall and leave it at that. It had to gloat: 'The next eastward bound freight train carried an old man, without shirt studs or other ornament, apparently bowed down by overwhelming grief, and the conductor hadn't the heart to throw him overboard. Gov Carney is not buying bones and hides in this city any more.'

POKER MERCENARY

VIRGINIA, 1878

Mercenary soldiers are for hire in times of war, and football clubs buy players in to improve their teams, but it is rare for poker players to be enticed into a game for the benefit of a cause with which they would otherwise have little sympathy.

So, this example of a poker mercenary rushing to the aid of a struggling team may be unique in the annals of nineteenth-century poker.

But as it was recorded in some detail by a newspaper called the *Argonaut* on 23 March 1878, we are entitled to accept the veracity of the incident, which involved a poker showdown between players from Virginia City and their counterparts in Carson City.

Rivalry between the two communities over the relative abilities of their top gambling men had been hostile for many years. Virginia were grudgingly believed to have a slight edge when the game being played was Faro, but Carson's boys were said to be tops at draw poker.

Now, though, Virginia were in town to take the poker honours. However, things were not going too well – to the extent that their leader, Billy Robinson, had to wire to the team's financial backers at the Delta Saloon that they should 'Send down $500 by telegraph'. An hour later another message was sent: 'Send $1,000 more – and Joe Dixon'.

Dixon was to deliver the money by horse, but before setting off he hit on an idea and sent off a Western Union dispatch to an acquaintance, professional poker player Charles Huntley, requesting that he 'meet me at Ormsby House. Business – Dixon'. Dixon set off for Carson, arriving there at around midnight with the cash that enabled the struggling Virginians to keep the game going for a while longer.

But at 2 a.m. a crucial hand worth $1,500 went Carson's way. In desperation, more messages were sent and as a final throw of the dice, or shuffle of the cards, Virginia's backers approved a final input of $10,000 to the game.

At just after 3 a.m., Charles Huntley showed up. Reported the *Argonaut*:

> Huntley slid into the game like a phantom. He showed the requisite amount of coin, and the Carsonites laughed inwardly because they had another victim. He looked like a divinity student. When he dealt, his thin hands played like lightning over the pack; his shuffle was the work of a magician, and the cards seemed alive.
>
> Suddenly every player seemed extraordinarily proud of his hand and the raises mounted precipitously. When a Carson City player shoved a high stack of coins into the pot and murmured, 'I'll go two thousand better,' a hush fell on the table, but everyone saw the raise around to Huntley, who hesitated not for a second. 'And five thousand more,' he said, increasing the fortune piled in the middle of the table by that amount.
>
> There was a long pause, and then, one by one, the players threw in their cards. The Carson City men stood up and wandered toward the door. The game was over and Virginia City had won.
>
> Dixon scooped the big pot into an oversized bag and, grinning, shook hands all around – 'Say, Charlie,' Dixon asked, 'what did you have?'
>
> 'Don't know,' answered Huntley. 'To tell the truth, I haven't yet looked at my hand. If a man looks at his hands, sometimes he gets confused and loses his nerve. I believe largely in the straight bluff.'

However much the Virginians paid him, it wasn't enough!

BETWEEN GOD AND THE DEVIL

DENVER, 1878

Pap Wyman's 'Wild West' gambling and poker house in Leadville, Denver, had in 1878 a 'well-thumbed' Bible prominently displayed at its entrance.

This hostelry may well have been the one in which a sign was posted outlining the rules of the house. The actual identity of the venue seems to have been lost in the mists of poker history, but the rules survive and make for intriguing reading:

A club member must be a gentleman.
A gentleman plays according to the rules:
1. Watch your language
2. Pass, call, check and bet in turn
3. Show one – show all
4. Do not show your cards until play is completed
5. All checked and called hands must be placed on the table – FIVE CARDS faced up
6. No talking about the hand or the plays if you are out of the pot (until play is completed)
7. No rabbit hunting
8. Announce all raises and the amount of the raise
9. Dealers must not look at top cards – at any time
10. No sharking
11. No string bets
12. No automatic insurance
13. In stud poker the dealer must deal the first card down
14. No looking at the deadwood at any time

$150,000 WEED KILLER

SOMEWHERE IN AMERICA, 1881

Heaven only knows what you could buy for $150,000 in 1881. One man, though, was in a position to know, after winning that amount in what its chronicler, the anonymous author of the contemporary book *Poker: How To Play It* published just one year later, declared, 'transcends anything heretofore known in America'. (Remember when reading this that the ranking of hands has changed over the years.)

'The parties engaged in the game were Francis P Weed, the victim, Dr Montreville M Hedges, and William M Scott, and they surrounded the festive card table, and in the exhilarating game of Draw Poker struggled with each other for the mastery and the "pots".'

It is not stated where the game was carried on, but rumour says it was 'in the private office of one of them'.

On the fateful hand, betting began with a thousand dollars, all three players believing they had strong hands. When betting reached $15,000, Weed supposedly said it was 'no use going any higher, boys; you haven't got the money to lose'. Scott retorted that he had property and could give security for as much as he wanted to bet.

So betting continued and before long the pot was at $150,000 and the call was made.

'When the hands were thrown down they quickly showed that Weed was the loser. Scott had drawn a straight flush, with king high; Weed added a fourth ace to the three he kept, and Hedges drew out a full hand.'

45

Interestingly, when I endeavoured to track down details of these poker players I discovered that on 4 March 1872 a Francis P Weed was dismissed from the membership of the Calvary Presbyterian Church at Newburgh, New York – the very same place from which on 5 December 1869 Mrs Frances P Weed had also been dismissed.

I wonder why!

A CHEAT – BUT A DIAMOND GEEZER

MISSISSIPPI, 1887

George Devol was a legendary card sharp, who plied his dubious trade on the American riverboats, fleecing suckers, out-hustling hustlers and conning the best conmen. He began his career at the age of ten in 1839, won and lost millions of dollars, and died with nothing in 1903.

Along the way, though, he lived life to the full and left behind him his 1887 memoirs, *Forty Years a Gambler on the Mississippi*, the majority of which tales show him getting the better of his opponents and displaying no remorse or regret. Yet, just once, the mask slips and he shows himself to be only human, after all.

I was playing poker with a gentleman on board the steamer *John Simmonds* bound for Louisville, late one night, and had won a few hundred dollars from him, when he got up without saying a word, and went to the ladies' cabin.

In a short time he came back with a small velvet-covered box in his hand, and said to me: 'Come, let us finish our game.' He opened the box and I saw it was full of ladies' diamond jewellery. I said, 'What are you going to do with those?' Said he, 'I will put them up as money.'

'Oh, no; I have no use for ladies' jewellery.'

'Well,' says he, 'if I lose I will redeem them when we get to Louisville.' I told him I was not going above Vicksburg. 'Well,' says he, 'if you win, leave them with the clerk and I will pay him.'

47

I then loaned him $1,500 on the jewellery and we sat down to play. It was about 3 a.m. when we commenced, and before they wanted the tables for breakfast I had won the $1,500 back. We drank a champagne cocktail and he went to his room.

The barber was at work on me, so that I was a little late for breakfast, and the steward had to take me into the ladies' cabin to get me a seat.

There was a gentleman, a very beautiful lady, and a sweet little child at the same table; the lady's eyes were red as if she had been crying. I looked at the gentleman, and saw it was the same person who had lost the diamonds. Somehow, my breakfast did not suit me; and the more I looked at that young wife and mother, the less I felt like eating. So at last I got up and left the table. I went to my room, got the little velvet box, wrapped it up, and carried it back.

They were just leaving the table when I returned. I called the chambermaid and told her the lady had left a package, and for her to take it to her room.

After it was gone I felt better, and I ate a square meal. The gentleman came and thanked me, and wanted my address; but as I never had any one to send me money lost at gambling, I told him not to mind the address; for I knew if I did not give it, I would not expect anything and therefore would not be disappointed.

PRESIDENTIAL TREASURE

WHITE HOUSE, 1888

President Grover Cleveland was coming towards the end of his term of office, having been elected in 1885, when he played in a poker match against the Speaker of the House, John Griffin Carlisle.

The game's twists and turns were recorded for posterity by Southern journalist and politician Henry Watterson, who reported that the president was so impressed when Carlisle won a hand that he promised him a top job if he ever returned to the highest office in the land.

Also taking part in the poker game were secretary of the navy, Whitney, Senator Don Cameron of Pennsylvania and Watterson himself, who recalled: 'It chanced on a deal that I picked up a pat flush, Mr Cleveland a pat full. The Pennsylvania Senator and I went to the extreme, the President of course willing enough for us to lay his hand for him.'

The Speaker of the House, despite the heavy betting, stayed in the hand to the others' surprise. At the draw, Cameron drew one card, Cleveland stood pat and Carlisle drew four cards. When it came to the showdown, amazingly he held four kings.

'Take the money, Carlisle, take the money,' said the president. 'If ever I am president again you shall be secretary of the treasury. But don't you make that four-card draw too often.'

Indeed, Cleveland was to become president again – and Carlisle was, indeed, secretary of the treasury.

49

'RAISE YOU NEW MEXICO'

SANTA FE, 1889

The final raise in a bitterly fought game that took place in Santa Fe, New Mexico in 1889 might just have been the greatest in the entire history of poker.

The game was played in Bowen's Saloon and involved a cattle baron, Ike Jackson, from Colorado City in Texas and a resourceful professional gambler named Johnny Dougherty.

The match was always expected to be eventful and was being played in the presence of the governor, L Bradford Prince, and some one hundred of the area's most prominent citizens, for what was billed as the 'Championship Series of Poker'.

As the game proceeded, there was $100,000 on the table as a vital hand was played out.

Jackson had run out of cash, but wrote out a deed to his ranch, along with its 10,000 cattle, to bet with.

Dougherty was momentarily stumped as to how to respond to this enormous raise, but called for pen and paper himself, and promptly scribbled out some lines – which he handed to the governor, at the same time as he pulled a revolver on him and demanded: 'Governor, sign this – or I'll kill you.'

The New Mexican Governor did not even bother to read what he was signing but immediately put his mark on the document and handed it back.

Dougherty immediately threw the paper into the pot, saying, 'I raise you the Territory of New Mexico. There's the deed.'

Jackson knew when he was beaten and promptly threw in his hand.

ADVICE FROM ANOTHER CENTURY

USA, 1890

Shakespearean actor William J Florence's thespian abilities remain largely undebated, relegated to obscure corners of the theatrical world's historical chroniclers – whether his Hamlet outclassed his Bottom will perhaps never be known.

But while he was treading the boards in the States in the latter years of the nineteenth century, he accepted a wager that resulted in his name achieving some kind of immortality among poker players and gamblers.

In order to win the bet, whose stake is unknown, he had to compile within one month of 1890 the material for the book *The Gentlemen's Handbook on Poker*, which became one of the first 'How to . . .' or 'Teach yourself . . .' manuals on the increasingly popular game.

Just how much Florence knew about poker is also open to debate, but it is well worth revisiting the book, just to see how much the prevailing wisdom about poker and how to play it has changed – or not.

Florence included a chapter of 'Advice to Players' in the book:

The strong point in poker is never to lose your temper, either with those you are playing with or more particularly with the cards. There is no sympathy at poker. Always keep cool. If you lose your head you will lose all your chips. Poker being as much a criterion of character as anything else, keep in the shade your personalities . . .

51

Always believe in the equalization of chances. If your king flush is beaten twice hand running by an ace flush today, tomorrow you will hold the ace flushes and your adversaries the king flushes. If you begin to draw for flushes and straights and cannot fill them, you must continue trying to fill them, otherwise you throw away your chance of equalizing your draw.

To adhere to anything but the strictly truthful brings with poker no moral obliquity. As it is impossible for some players not to lie when they play, this want of veracity brings its own cure. It is not, however, a good rule to tell stories about your hand. You may, if you have the talent for such things, assume an innocent guise with your face alone. This is the most effective of lures. It is best never to show your hand at all, if not called, and to remain silent in regard to its merits. A solemn mystery to your cards is the most effective.

OK, ladies and gentleman, give it up for Mr Florence, let's hear it for William J – the poker-playing thespian.

All right, all right, an encore it is: 'Never play poker without a limit. It is then the most dangerous of all games.'

Thank you and goodnight, William J Florence.

POKER TOM IN A STEW

CALIFORNIA, 1891

In 1891 there occurred a poker game that, according to the 1978 Time Life book *The Gamblers*, 'precipitated a rare and bizarre case of murder and mayhem'.

One April evening, goes the story, a successful merchant from Bridgeport, California, a Chinese man called Ah Tia, became involved in a poker game with a group of Native Americans, among them an acknowledged crack player called Poker Tom.

Tom duly beat Ah Tia to the tune of some $200, whereupon he decided to quit the game. Ah Tia demanded that the game be reconvened the next evening to give him a chance of recouping his losses.

When Poker Tom's friends arrived the next evening they saw through the window that Tom was already there playing against Ah Tia on a head-to-head basis, so they left.

How it happened, and what incident during the game had prompted it, is not known, but it seems likely that as Poker Tom carried on winning, Ah Tia set upon him and slew him, dismembering the body, placing the arms and legs in a vat of brine and chopping the heart, liver and other organs into small pieces which he threw into a boiling cauldron already containing carrots and onions.

Ah Tia added a hint of soy sauce.

He disposed of the remainder of Tom's body by stuffing the parts into a trunk and throwing it into the West Walker River. He took Poker Tom's arms and legs and cut them into chop-sized pieces, which he sold from his store as goat meat at six cents per pound.

He then invited Poker Tom's friends, who presumably were at that time unaware of his demise, to share a dinner of stew with him.

When the trunk and a number of Tom's possessions were later discovered an inquest was held and Ah Tia duly charged with murder. The businessman could afford good legal representation and was acquitted by the presiding judge.

However, Poker Tom's friends were waiting to dispense their own justice and charged into the courtroom, grabbing the Chinaman, throwing him to the ground, roping his ankles and dragging him behind a horse to a patch of ground at the edge of town, where he breathed his last.

PROSPERING CHEATS

NEW YORK, 1894

'I have invented a process by which a man is sure of winning if he can introduce his own cards,' declared the author of a catalogue made available to those wishing to cheat at poker in 1894.

Produced by a firm in the state of New York, the catalogue purported to be of interest 'To Smart Poker Players' and had come to the attention of John Nevil Maskelyne, a man whose work in life was to expose crooked and shady practices employed by those involved in the gambling world.

Maskelyne's book, *Sharps and Flats* was extremely successful when it appeared and was followed eight months later by another.

Exposing the 'invention' aimed at unscrupulous poker cheats, the catalogue item continued: 'The cards are not trimmed or marked in any way, shape or manner. They can be handled and shuffled by all at the board, and, without looking at a card you can, by making two or three shuffles or ripping them in, oblige the dealer to give three of a kind to any one playing, or the same advantage can be taken on your own deal.'

The catalogue boasts of the high quality of the cards, insisting that the preparation used will 'last as long as the cards do. The object is to make certain cards, not prepared, slip off easier than others in shuffling.'

All this for the princely sum of $2 per pack, or a dozen for $20

Maskelyne was in no doubt about the morals of this trader –

'The fact that these people should be allowed to carry on their trade in the way they do is nothing short of a standing disgrace in America and a satire upon civilisation.'

And of course no specially created cheating implements are available today . . . are they?!

THE LOLLAPALOOZA HAND

MONTANA, 1896

This story has assumed mythical status today, but was first told to the world in 1896 by John F B Lillard, in a book entitled *Poker Stories*.

The cautionary tale is set in Butte, Montana, in a saloon where four hard-bitten prospectors are playing draw poker.

Enter a card sharp, who asked whether he could join the game.

'Sure, sit down, stranger,' nodded one of the prospectors.

After playing for an hour or so the sharp stacked the cards and dealt himself four aces. He made a fair-sized bet, and everybody dropped out, except for one old-timer with grey whiskers and a deadpan, poker face.

At the draw, both stood pat. The sharper counted the prospector's cash and bet an equal amount.

The old boy didn't bat an eyelid. He shoved all of his chips into the pot and called.

The sharp exultantly spread his four aces on the table and reached for the pot.

'Not so fast, sonny,' said the old boy, laying down three clubs and two diamonds.

'What do you mean, not so fast?' said the shocked sharper. 'I've got four aces.'

'Sure you do – but in this town a Lollapalooza beats any other poker hand. And that's what I've got – three clubs and two diamonds.'

The other prospectors nodded solemnly, backing him up.

'That's right, stranger – nothing beats a Lollapalooza.'

The sharp knew he had been cheated but figured he had an answer. On his next deal he stacked the cards again, this time dealing himself a Lollapalooza and making sure the old boy had four aces in his hand.

Again, the sharp made a fair-sized bet and again the old boy stayed in, the others dropping out. Once more both men stood pat on the draw, the sharper pushed in all of his chips and the prospector called him.

'Well,' said the grinning sharp, 'this time I can't lose – I've got the Lollapalooza.'

The prospector reached over and raked in the pot: 'Sorry, pardner. You should be sure of the rules before you play. The Lollapalooza hand can only be played once a night.'

The other prospectors nodded sagely.

TALE OF A CORNY KIND

MISSISSIPPI, 1896

'I was on one of the smaller boats one night on which were some gamblers going down the river to meet a large steamer coming up,' recorded John F B Lillard in his 1896 book *Poker Stories*.

I suppose the partners on the big boat had most of their gambling machinery. At any rate, when they saw two or three young plantation men on the boat they could only find one greasy pack of cards and no chips. The boat had a cargo of corn, so one of the party shelled some and it was used as chips.

About the time this decision was made one of the planters disappeared. He had managed to slip down into the hold where the corn was, and in the dark he took the first ear he found, and, shelling it, put the corn in his pocket. He afterward joined the game, buying some chips, which he placed in another pocket.

Luck was against him, and he lost his last honest chip. It was his turn to ante. He plunged his hand down into his pocket, got some grains of corn, and slapped them down on the table. When he raised his hand, lo and behold, the grains were red. In an instant every man was on his feet. One held a pistol at his head, while the rest went through his pockets. Of course they brought up a whole lot of red corn. The corn that the dealers had shelled and given out was white. They bound him hand and foot, and were

59

holding a council to determine what to do with him when we heard the whistle of the big steamer.

They took him on board with them, and I never could learn what they did with him, but I was on the river for many years after that and I never saw him again.

NOME, SWEET NOME

NOME, 1897

Known as 'Swiftwater' because of his fear of fast-flowing water, William F Gates, a short, but heavily bearded man, was a successful poker player during the Klondike gold rush. His talents were eventually given a wider audience when Jed Jordan, owner of the Ophir Saloon in Nome, Alaska, wrote about him in the book *Fool's Gold*.

'In a poker game he was ruthless. If his grandmother was holding a pair of tens and he had four aces he would sandbag her.'

But Jordan also felt that Gates had a touch of 'poker genius' about him and illustrated the point in a fascinating description of an 1897 game in the Ophir in which Gates was 'sitting in a seven-handed draw game with two strangers, one on his left, the other on his right'.

Explained Jordan:

The stranger on his right was dealing when Bill got four aces on the draw. This miracle would have made most people suspicious (it was not an unbeatable hand at the time but old Bill was as happy as a Cheechako). There was considerable betting around the table and the pot mounted to around $1,000. Bill shoved his entire stack into the game.

Just at this moment, right before the draw, one of the strangers upset his drink. I happened to be looking straight at the dealer at the time and I saw him milk the cards. Everybody in the game had turned to help mop up the spilled drink.

Swiftwater Bill put down his hand, covered it with his pipe and came over to the bar. He was in danger of being frozen out and he wanted me to lend him some money.

'That fellow is milking,' I whispered to him.

'Jed, you are a cynical man,' Swiftwater Bill said blithely. 'I have a good hand and that fellow would not hustle. Is my credit good for $500?'

He went back to the table and threw the entire $500 into the pot as a raise. Each of the two strangers met the bet. Everybody else was out of the game.

Then came the draw. Bill was holding four aces. He could either draw one card or stand pat. What did he do? He threw away two of his aces and a third card, held on to his remaining pair and asked for three cards.

In the showdown he won the pot. On a pair of aces. It amounted to about $2,500.

Bill had figured out what I couldn't see.

If the game was fixed, the only hand that could beat him was a straight flush, and that would have to be held by the player on his left. Bill could not improve his hand, but the man on his left could. Therefore, Bill reasoned, the fellow on the left was holding, say, the six, seven, eight and nine of spades, because the dealer could not have dared hand him a pat straight flush, not with four aces already being dealt out. When the dealer milked the cards he transferred the five and ten of spades from the bottom to the top of the deck.

If Bill took one card, the opponent on his left would get the five of spades. If Bill stood pat, the man would get the ten.

The cheats could not lose. Either way, the fellow filled his straight flush.

Except that Bill broke up his fours and took three cards and raised the deal.

POKER MANNERS – ACCORDING TO MADGE

LONDON, 1897

'Billiards, backgammon, poker, bezique, baccarat, ecarte, draughts, vingt-et-un, and loo may be mentioned among the minor accomplishments with which the modern young man finds it convenient to be equipped,' declared Mrs Humphry, also known as 'Madge' from *Truth*, presumably a magazine of its day, when in 1897 London publisher James Bowden issued her book *Manners for Men*.

The book saw Mrs Humphry advising on the correct etiquette for any amount of social situations, not the least the poker table and its environs.

She was, though, somewhat concerned 'that a bad use has been made of some of those (games) by converting them into media for gambling'.

Mrs Humphry advised that 'the demeanour of a young man when playing cards affords a very good test of his manners' but was shocked that 'some of them appear to think that the only fun to be had out of the game lies in cheating – very open and transparent cheating to be sure – but still sufficient to spoil the amusement of others.'

Nor were all of those whom Mrs Humphry was hoping to improve in their manners good losers at the poker table, as she noticed 'a curious development of money greed in players, who will show extreme exasperation at the loss of so simple a coin as a penny'.

But Mrs Humphry was only too aware of the danger of the

unwary poker player being led astray: 'It is possible for a young man, being unaware of the fact, to be drawn in and lose more than he can afford before he can politely extricate himself.'

But what to do, if so caught?

'The only thing he can do is religiously to avoid any such house in future. It is a matter of notoriety that there are men who make good incomes by fleecing the young and inexperienced whom they invite to their houses under the guise of friendship.'

And, lest readers believe such things went on only in the dens of iniquity to be found in big cities, Mrs H warned: 'The matter is not confined to London; country-house life has much to answer for under the same heading.'

For 1897, read 2007!

POKER'S MOST VALUABLE ANTIQUE

MANHATTAN, TURN OF THE 20TH CENTURY

A huge bronze door was installed to protect the Doge's wine cellar in Venice at the end of the fifteenth century.

It was a tremendous piece of work that, some four hundred years later, was purchased at a cost of $20,000 and installed in the gambling club on Manhattan's West 33rd Street by owner Frank Farrell, a well-heeled, well-connected figure in the shadowy gambling world, who needed the kind of door that would protect his patrons from the occasional police raid.

'Gamblers loved the relative security of Farrell's club,' recalls Bristol-based antiques dealer Michael Wright, who has a special interest in the bronze door. 'He built an enormous fortune by offering poker players a secure environment. In many respects it's a bit like an online poker room offering a secure server to today's players.'

The bronze door repaid its huge cost when it repelled a police raid by DA William Travers Jerome and his men, who used blowtorches and other devices, but were held back for long enough to enable the wealthy and influential poker players to make good their escapes.

The door's whereabouts are now unknown, but Wright has been hired by a gaming memorabilia enthusiast to track it down – and Wright knows it is worth tracking down. 'Given its history it is worth perhaps $450,000 depending upon its present condition.'

Wright has drawn a blank in his American searches and

65

believes the door may now be somewhere in Europe, so keep an eye out when you are scrabbling around antique markets, boot sales and the like – just in case.

DOWN TO THE BARE BONES

MONTY'S PLACE, INDIANA, C. 1905

Herbert O Yardley's 1957 book *The Education of a Poker Player* is widely regarded as an all-time classic of the genre.

Published a year before he died, Yardley included a string of classic yarns, witnessed personally during his days as a player, none more dramatic and tragic than when he saw 'the big Swede, Bones Alverson, a poor weather-beaten corn farmer, bet the last of his farm against a tent show'.

Born in 1889, Yardley became fascinated by poker when, aged sixteen, he began to hang around Monty's Place, one of seven saloons in the little Indiana frontier town where he had grown up.

Monty's Place had exerted its influence over Yardley 'because it offered more colour and action'.

Yardley had quickly been accepted by those who played at Monty's, and he was sitting in on a game one evening along with the eponymous owner of Monty's and two new players, both thespians: actor Tom Lawrence and producer Pete Hunter. Also in the game were 'Chic', 'Doc' and Bones Alverson, the farmer who had already gambled away 'most of his farm' at the poker table.

Alverson hit a winning streak as they played five-card draw, deuces wild.

There came a hand in which Alverson came in for $50. Monty folded. Lawrence threw his cards in, but Hunter raised $100. Yardley folded, as did both Chic and Doc.

Bones studied his hand then pushed in a stack of chips. 'I up you five hundred.'

The producer was unfazed: 'I'm just going to raise you five hundred.'

'Five hundred more,' declared Bones – swearing at his opponent for good measure.

But Bones didn't have the cash and asked Monty to stake him, saying, 'You've never seen me welch on a bet.'

That much was true. Monty asked after Bones's farm. Alverson admitted that $15,000 of the $20,000 value of his farm and its equipment was owed to a land speculator, Bert Wills, but added, 'I have five thousand equity.'

Monty warned Bones not to risk the remainder of what he owned, but the Swede was adamant: 'I might just as well be broke as to try to pay ten per cent interest on $15,000 to that goddamned bloodsucker.'

Monty accepted Alverson's IOU and threw $1,000 into the pot for him.

The producer looked thoughtfully at his hand. It was his turn to consider his options. He paid in $500 in $100 bills then announced that he intended to raise Bones $2,000, but 'I'll have to give you an IOU'.

This did not go down well with the Swede, who demanded, 'Put up, or shut up.'

Now the producer played the 'Monty' card, asking him to take the IOU. Monty declined.

Hunter and Lawrence conferred and came up with a proposition. Monty should put the Bones IOU into the pot and take out his money. The producer would then put in a bill of sale for his travelling theatrical 'tent show', valued at $2,000, while Bones should make out a similar bill of sale for his farm – including the debt on it – worth $3,000. 'The extra thousand covers the money you take from the pot,' said Hunter.

Monty had the bills of sale drawn up – they all signed and the game continued, with Bones drawing one card – but as it was passed over to him by Doc, who was dealing, it turned face up, revealing itself to be a wild card. But, under house rules, that deal was now void as a result of the card being exposed, and the deal now passed to the producer before returning to Bones.

Bones was devastated as the wild card would clearly have

given him the advantage. He made as if to protest, but 'fell over the table, clutching the cards in a heavy fist'.

He was dead.

The producer moved to rake in the cash – but Monty thrust out a hand to stop him.

'But it's mine,' said the producer.

'Not yet,' said Monty, 'I think he had you beat. He didn't need the joker.'

The producer disagreed and demanded to be allowed to make his draw. Monty agreed, provided that Bones's hand could then be played on his behalf.

The producer took one and Yardley played the Bones hand, which had by now been prised from his lifeless fist. He took one card.

The producer showed his hand – queen, king, king, king, deuce (wild) – four kings.

Yardley described the climax. 'Doc turned over Bones's cards one at a time – ace, ace, ace, jack . . . deuce (wild) – four aces.'

Monty now added the postscript as he gathered up the money – 'I'll take this to Bones's widow. She'll probably grieve a couple of days, then be relieved that he's dead – at least he can't gamble the farm away now.'

The producer told Monty he would redeem the tent show bill of sale when the banks opened. 'You will like hell. I'll redeem it myself. I've always wanted to go into show business.'

THAT MUST HAVE BEEN MURDER

NEW YORK, 1906

It was the most scandalous crime of 1906. And it was committed by a poker man. Harry Kendall Thaw, who claimed that during his Harvard career he 'studied poker', murdered high-profile architect Stanford White with three shots to the face.

Born in 1871, Thaw, a very wealthy fellow, heir to a multimillion-dollar mine and railroad fortune, and a copious user of drugs, had another poker claim to fame, having once played for a reported record-beating continuous 62 hours at the old Metropole Hotel – in the process losing $185,000.

The fatal attack took place after Thaw and White, who shared a mutual 'hobby' of studying chorus girls, both became desirous of the attentions of one Evelyn Nesbit, a chorus girl in the hit show of the day, *Floradora*.

She was playing one off against the other and Thaw proposed to her. She turned him down and apparently indicated that she had lost her honour to White, which enraged Thaw, who beat her with a dog whip.

Obsessed by her, Thaw finally persuaded her to marry him – immediately after which ceremony he began to go off her.

In the spring of 1906 Evelyn and Harry ran into Stanford White while out dining. Discovering that White was preparing to visit the premiere of a show called *Mamzelle Champagne* at the rooftop theatre of Madison Square Garden, Thaw took Evelyn home to change, and they then returned to the theatre. During the show's finale, 'I Could Love a Million Girls', Thaw left Evelyn, approached White's table and shot him at close range. He then held the gun aloft and walked through the crowd of people to meet up with Evelyn at the elevator.

Thaw stood trial twice for the murder. The first produced a deadlocked jury. At the second he was pleading insanity, but was astonishingly declared not guilty, on the grounds that he had suffered from a 'brainstorm'.

Thaw was, though, incarcerated at an asylum for the criminally insane. He walked out of there in 1913 and in 1915 was ruled to be sane. He then divorced Evelyn.

In 1917 he was again declared insane and sent to an asylum for seven years, being allowed out in 1924.

He died of a heart attack in 1947 and left $10,000 to Evelyn Nesbit in his will, a sum worth one hundred times that amount today.

POKER PROS FOOLED

ARIZONA, 1907

Poker was banned along with other gambling games when on 1 April 1907 – the date may have been a symbolic gesture – stringent anti-gambling measures were put into place in Arizona.

And the move received conditional support from the media – if tinged with a touch of regret.

For example, the *Phoenix Gazette* reported: 'Both the city and the Territory have refused the gamblers any further privileges and, like the Wandering Jew, they were told to move on. The men who operated these games in Phoenix are, as a rule, good men; probably the squarest games in Arizona were those operated in this city.'

Century Magazine quoted the response of one of the banned gamblers: 'This place is dead now. Every man, woman and beast goes to bed at eight o'clock. Sleeping has become one of our principal industries.'

Another pointed out that gambling would now go underground and, as he said, 'You've got to give up more than half you make to the graft; you've got to take all sorts of insults from the tenderfoots without even pulling a gun. You're no more than a pickpocket or a sneak-thief in the eye of the law.'

The *Tombstone Prospector* declared: 'Since Tombstone's inception the most noted sporting men of the United States came and went and returned . . . This was a veritable Mecca for them. They prospered and lent valuable aid in opening up the country.'

The *Prescott Journal-Miner* spoke of the gamblers as 'Tigers' and noted, 'Unscrupulous ones there were among them, 'tis true, e'en as there are in every walk of life, but the majority, at least, were and are men with the making of good citizens; men who, on the whole, lived good clean lives; men whom but few were ashamed to extend the right hand of fellowship.'

WELL-TRAINED CHEATS

NEBRASKA, 1910

The railroads were instrumental in permitting early travellers to move around the vast expanses of America – but some of those travellers found themselves exposed to unexpected perils.

In 1910, the respected publication *Harper's Magazine* carried an article by writer George Jean Nathan; he had interviewed an unnamed gambler who was working the trains in Nebraska.

He was, wrote Nathan, 'a grey-haired, pleasant-faced man of about 48, one of the most famous gamblers of his day in the Western States'.

Frustrating though it is not to know the man's identity, his bona fides can be taken as read, and he explained, 'Poker was our game, not three-card monte as you might suppose.' He worked with two accomplices, he went on. They would identify a likely victim, start a game nearby and gradually tempt him in, before accusing him of cheating and 'finding' a card hidden about his person. They would then brand him a proven cheat and relieve him of the cash they said he must have come by via nefarious means.

This was a surprisingly lucrative trade. 'On one of the Denver trains, worked by another gambler and myself, we cleaned up $30,000 in six months. $5,000 of this amount we got by luring two men into a big-stake game and holding them up with revolvers.'

AND YOU THOUGHT IT WAS JUST A GAME OF CARDS!

CANTON, OHIO, 1912

Poker threatened the very future of the country, warned a reformed American professional gambler in 1912, in a book 'designed to instruct the youth of the world to avoid all forms of gambling'.

John Philip Quinn had reached his 67th year, during which time he had spent one quarter-century period witnessing and practising 'every variety of gambling known to the profession' and the next 25-year spell 'devoted to exposing the frauds of the gambler'.

And Quinn was in no doubt as to the blackest and bleakest threat to the nation – poker: 'This game sanctioned as it practically is, by the countenance of the reputable men who never set foot within a gambling house, has done more to weaken the moral sense of the country at large as to the general question of gambling than any other single agency.'

He went on to lament the threat to nation's morals and prosperity. 'A nation of gamblers is a nation whose course is already turned towards the setting sun.'

Quinn was particularly concerned at poker's ability to appeal to otherwise respectable folk, thus insidiously corrupting them. 'Gentlemen, who would not, for worlds, enter a gaming hell . . . play poker at their clubs and by their own firesides, without either compunction of conscience or pretence of concealment.'

Quinn launched his 'Anti-Gambling Crusade' for which he was seeking 7,500 like-minded people to shell out a dollar to

75

join up. 'To describe its fascination is as difficult as to account for it, yet the undisputable fact remains that of the vast army of men connected with mercantile pursuits in the United States, comparatively few can be found who have not some knowledge of the game.'

Nothing worse than a chap who has finally seen the light, wouldn't you say?

THREE STEPS TO POKER HEAVEN

LONDON, 1920

R F Foster had come up with the three vital elements for success at the game of poker, he believed. And he decided to share them with the good folk of Britain – at a price.

As it was 1920, that price was a relatively substantial 'one shilling' – a mere 5p in today's currency.

Foster's findings appeared in a small, red-covered volume, published by Thos. De La Rue & Co Ltd of London. And he summed them up in a few words: 'control your features, vary your play, and never lay odds against yourself'.

Of course, he couldn't just leave it at that or he wouldn't have made many shillings. So further elucidation on each of these points was forthcoming:

SELF-CONTROL is undoubtedly the most important element of success, because the slightest exhibition of joy or disappointment, of confidence or fear, will at once betray you to a watchful opponent. Those who can simulate these emotions are not half so successful as those who can preserve a perfectly impassable countenance. Of all things, the beginner should avoid undue haste with good hands and unnecessary deliberation with doubtful ones. It is an excellent plan to lay the cards upon the table, placing a counter upon them, so as to avoid any possible unconscious movement of the hands.

VARIETY OF PLAY [is] very important. The player who never comes in unless he can beat openers, who never raises before the draw unless he has aces or better, or who never does anything or always does something under the same circumstances is lost; because his adversaries will quickly discover his peculiarities and play accordingly.

BETTING AGAINST YOURSELF is one of the most common faults at Poker, even among players of experience. Every Poker player should know the chances of improving a given hand. By noting the amount in the pool at the time you are called upon to bet, and considering the probability of your being raised by players behind you, you can weigh your chances of making a wager in which you will have the odds in your favour instead of laying them against yourself.

Eighty-plus-year-old wisdom, maybe – but based on sound principles, for sure.

HOW MOSS'S MRS WAS LEFT
HOLDING THE BABY

TEXAS, 1925

Johnny Moss had learned how to play poker by the age of ten. He'd also decided how he would make his living when his father told him that he either had to give up work or give up gambling.

'But if I don't work how can I get money to gamble?' he asked his daddy. 'That's what gamblers got to figure out,' came the reply.

So, the young Texan quit work and decided to become a professional poker player.

Before hitting the road, and at the tender age of just eighteen in 1925, he wed childhood sweetheart Virgie Ann, who travelled along with him, keeping tabs on their gambling money. On their wedding night Moss had played poker, and during the course of the game had been losing so badly that he had to 'borrow' his new wife's engagement ring to stake another hand – she gave it up voluntarily. 'If I hadn't Johnny would have ripped my whole finger off.' The ring put Moss back on track in the game, and sixty years later she still had the engagement ring to show off while telling the story.

But as Johnny headed for the East Texas oilfields where he played poker 'with the roughnecks and the drillers', Virgie Ann became pregnant.

Johnny was already becoming worldly wise and realising that not everyone was happy being beaten by a greenhorn kid.

There were 'more cheaters than oil wells', discovered Johnny who was asked in one dodgy game, 'What do you have to take this pot?' to which he replied, 'Two sixes', pulling out just that – a pair of six-guns.

The arrival of the first Moss offspring was imminent, and Virgie Ann booked into a $35 room in the local hospital to prepare to give birth. Johnny saw her safely installed before popping out to play a pre-birth game of craps and a hand or two of poker.

He lost all their ready cash and had to head back to the hospital to take Virgie Ann back home as he could no longer afford to pay for her stay.

Their daughter, the interestingly named Eleoweese – 'My daddy gave Eleoweese her name; she must have been ten years old before I learned how to spell it' – was born at home with Moss acting as midwife to the doctor, who waived his $35 fee when Moss explained his lack of finances. Moss went to work as a security guard to earn the money to pay back the medic.

Still, Virgie Ann probably consoled herself, that's the worst he can do to me. Well . . .

Moss, then living in Dallas, decided he would spend a spectacular 1939 $250,000 winning poker hand on buying a new house. He sent Virgie Ann out to check out the local property market.

After a thorough search she came up with the ideal house for them, and happily told Moss the search was over. 'Sorry, but you looked too long,' he said, confessing he had lost the money.

Virgie then began to exercise more control over their finances and their position improved to the point that, in an effort to get him finally to settle down, he recalled, 'She said she'd pay me a thousand a week if I was to come and lie around the house in Odessa and drink whiskey all day.'

He was tempted, but then realised, 'What would I do with a thousand a week if I couldn't gamble?'

But he did go on to become the first man ever to win the World Championship of poker – the WSOP title – three times, securing poker immortality for himself.

THE RIDDLE OF BLUFFING

COLUMBIA, USA, 1925

Ethel M Riddle, a psychologist, decided to investigate the psychology of bluffing in poker by wiring a group of players up to lie detectors to gauge their reactions during a 1925 game.

Although the technology may have been in its infancy back then, Ms Riddle utilised breathing-measurement equipment to reveal the ways in which players were affected by the differing strategies they were using while playing.

She had put together a group of six relatively young students from Columbia, who took part in a poker game with a 5-cent ante and a 20-cent limit, paying them $1 per hour for taking part. The players all wore on their chests an instrument called a stethograph, whose purpose was to record respiratory movements. A team of lady volunteers was on hand to interpret the data gathered.

Ms Riddle was using the experiment as the basis of her PhD thesis, 'Aggressive Behaviour in a Small Social Group', which was languishing in the files of the Library of Congress when poker writer David Spanier unearthed it in the 1970s.

'She chose poker for her model because the number of players is small, each player can be easily observed, and in the form chosen, five-card stud, it is possible to determine the stimulus to each player, in his own hand and from his opponents', as each card falls or each bet is made.'

The group played 62 hands, during which each player was required to make a note every time they bluffed or believed another player was bluffing them.

81

Ultimately, once she had analysed her results, Ethel concluded that the optimum percentage of hands in which a player should bluff is 6 per cent. This percentage, she believed, 'renders the opponents less capable of judging when the player is bluffing and when not'.

She also observed that 'all the players were poor judges of when they were being bluffed' and that 'the winning player, or the one who bet the highest in the game, was the one whom the others most frequently tried to bluff out, and not the player who would be, in fact, the easiest to bluff.'

Spanier pondered Ms Riddle's work in his book *Total Poker*, and mused: 'Isn't it the high bettor, the swashbuckler, the come-and-get-me player whom one frequently tries to challenge at poker? And if so, why? Perhaps to bring him down, to show he's not going to have things all his own way; perhaps to assert oneself in the game.'

Ethel obviously impressed her examiners, as she was awarded her PhD – after which she abandoned psychological experiments.

UNIVERSITY POKER RACE

HARVARD, 1926

England's world famous University Boat Race, between Oxford and Cambridge, may have been the inspiration for a similarly hard-fought showdown

Between their American equivalents, Harvard and Yale.

But although the first glimmerings of such a contest may have been sparked in 1926, it was the best part of eighty years before they were acted upon.

It was poker writer George Coffin, author of *The Poker Game Complete*, who, in his book in the late 1940s wrote: 'In our Harvard College days in 1926, old landmark Beck Hall, long since replaced by a modern structure, commanded a fine quarter-mile view up Massachusetts Avenue to Harvard Square, the shopping hub of Cambridge, Mass. Whenever one student with rooms facing the square held a Poker game, he used to herald it by hanging a red lantern out of his window!'

One hopes there were no unfortunate misunderstandings in those days, given the differing symbolism of red lights in many places today.

Anyhow, there is no doubt that Harvard 'has a deeply embedded poker culture'. Michael Jordan of the University's humour magazine, *Lampoon*, told me so in early 2006. He also told me that 'Harvard is home to six poker societies and dozens of casual games'. However, 'because of local laws, there is no recognized poker society. So, many students play through poker websites.'

Perhaps, then, this is why in November 2005, 'The

83

Tournament' – contested by Harvard and Yale University student poker teams – was instigated, supported by Truepoker.com website.

And it is hoped that this will indeed become a tradition to rival the Boat Race – 'The Tournament is an annual event held between the two Ivy League powerhouses of poker during the weekend of The Game', a wider sporting set-to between the houses of learning.

Harvard came out on top of the inaugural event, with Jeremy Warshauer,a Harvard 'poker phenom' leading the team to triumph. Later, he won another online event through Truepoker – a trip to play in the World Series of Poker, even though at that point he had never visited Vegas and, at 19, was too young to set foot inside a casino.

So, as he could not take up his main prize, Warshauer was offered the cash equivalent for his seat – $10,000.

In his first year at Harvard, Warshauer had tried to start an official university poker club, 'but Harvard would not support it because the city of Cambridge, Mass does not allow games of chance.'

Michael Jordan is happy with the progress of the new tradition so far and expects its profile to be raised: 'As far as a schoolwide prize or trophy, Truepoker purchased an ad in the *Harvard Lampoon* in order to announce the winning school. Prizes may be expanded/altered in next year's tournament.'

And you would expect the beaten players at Yale – which was attended by currently successful poker player and author Matt Matros, whose *The Making of a Poker Player* became a 2005 best seller – to be plotting their revenge, even if everyone at the University may not be sure whether poker should be classed as a sport or a game. Writing for *The Yale Herald*, Alessandro Presti mused in October 2004, 'Poker does not entail feats of speed, strength or dexterity – at least in the physical sense . . . But let's put semantics aside for a second. If poker's not a sport, what is it doing on [TV channel] ESPN, the traditional bastion of such manly and mainstream sports as baseball, football and hockey? . . . Poker may not be a sport but it certainly embodies many of the fundamental qualities that define sport . . . Poker is inherently competitive, filled with pressure and, as with any mainstream sport, requires endless hours of practice and conditioning.'

A sport, then – just like rowing, but one now attracting attention from students regardless of which educational establishment they attend, hence the launch of the Annual College Poker Championship in 2004.

DON'T CALL ME CARD-FACE

LOUISIANA, C. 1927

Al Capone, the legendary gangster, born in January 1899 in Brooklyn, New York, grew up to take an iron grip on the underworld during the era of prohibition when, known as 'Scarface', he controlled speakeasies, gambling houses, racetracks, nightclubs, breweries and much more.

The mobster, who was run out of Chicago and moved to Florida in the late 1920s, also enjoyed playing poker – and one of his favourite locations for doing so was the Seelbach Hotel in Louisville, Kentucky, which, the establishment's own website boasts today, he 'used to visit frequently for blackjack, poker and bootlegging'.

The site informs us: 'Today, you can dine in a small alcove in The Oakroom where Capone would play cards.'

And it also gives an insight into how careful the gang leader had to be even while ostensibly relaxing over a hand or two of poker. 'The famous gangster even sent a large mirror from Chicago, still in the room today, so that he could watch his back!'

If the authorities were tipped off about his whereabouts, Capone was ready to throw his cards in and escape. 'Capone's favourite room has two hidden doors behind special panels, leading to secret passageways. If the police came on a raid, Capone could slip out the concealed passageways – one way led down to Fourth Street – another led to an alley out the back of the hotel. The room even had spring-loaded doors that would be quickly shut using a pedal by an outside guard, warning Capone of a raid.'

WHO SHOT A.R.?

NEW YORK, 1928

Arnold 'The Brain' Rothstein was not, perhaps, the most lovable man ever to play poker. Suspected by many to be the brains behind the infamous fixing of the 1919 World Series of baseball when a number of players went bent to ensure the Chicago White Sox lost to the underdogs, the Cincinnati Redlegs, he was an inveterate big-money poker hustler, credited with winning what was at the time said to be the largest ever single hand, worth $605,000, from infamous gambler Nick the Greek.

On 8 September 1928 (some reports say it was the 29th), Rothstein was invited to a high-stakes poker game organised by New York bookie George McManus, held in the Congress Apartment building (on the corner of 54th Street and 7th Avenue) home of gambler and former convict Jimmy Meehan, a pal of Rothstein.

Also in the game was inveterate gambler 'Titanic' Thompson and two of his long-term acquaintances from San Francisco, Joe Bernstein and Nate Raymond, the latter apparently on honeymoon, albeit he had left his actress bride behind in California.

Local high rollers Sol Fusik, Oscar Donnelly and Abe Silverman also sat in on the game, while other reports suggested brothers Meyer and Samuel Boston, and bookmaker Martin Bowe were present.

Rothstein was into a number of suspect operations, such as bootlegging, nightclubs and drug running, and it is said that both Damon Runyan – 'The Brain' – and Scott Fitzgerald – 'Wolfsheim' – immortalised him as characters in their books.

The game was to be five-card stud and it was not long before the stakes for each hand were running into thousands.

Rothstein began to lose. Apparently understaked with cash, he was covering his losing bets with 'markers' – the equivalent of IOUs.

As the game wound down, the final hand of what had apparently turned into a thirty-hour marathon saw Rothstein offering to cut the deck for a high card against Nate for the modest consideration of $40,000.

'Don't appear to be your night, Mr Rothstein,' declared Nate as the cards were revealed.

As losses and winnings were tallied up it seemed that Rothstein owed Nate $319,000; Bernstein $69,000; Fusik $29,000; Donnelly $20,000; Silverman $8,000; and Thompson $30,000 – which all added up to $475,000.

It wasn't all bad news for Rothstein, though – he had at least managed to win $51,000 from McManus, who promptly settled up in cash.

Rothstein left the game, promising to pay his debts within days, saying, 'I'm Rothstein, that name ought to be good for the money.'

Days passed, then weeks. There was no settlement, and rumours began to circulate that Rothstein was alleging the game had been crooked. He was, though, said to have told Runyon that he was just making them sweat a little by having to wait.

Silverman, albeit having the least to collect, made a scene in public when he bumped into Rothstein, and was told to come to Rothstein's office for his money. It was said a Chicago gang had been hired to collect or to rub Rothstein out. Police later said that he had decided, 'I'm not going to give them a cent, and that goes for the gamblers and the gorillas.'

On the evening of 4 November, at around 10.15 p.m., Rothstein visited his favourite restaurant, Lindy's, where he received a phone call from George McManus, organiser of the poker school, asking Rothstein to come to room 349 at the Park

Central Hotel where he hoped to broker a deal over the payment of Rothstein's debts.

Rothstein set off to walk there, but at 11.07 p.m. was found in the 56th Street service area of the hotel, suffering from a bullet wound to the groin. Despite asking for a doctor and a taxi, he was rushed to Polyclinic Hospital, still conscious but either unable or unwilling to name his attacker, declaring, 'I got nothing to say. I won't talk about it.'

At 10.15 a.m. on 6 November, election day, he died, aged 46. When the election result was known, with Herbert Hoover winning, bets Rothstein had made worth $500,000 had proved successful. His death voided the bets.

George McManus was indicted for murdering Rothstein and brought to trial a year later, but the prosecution had no eyewitnesses and McManus was acquitted.

The case remained 'open' according to NYPD records for many years to come, but those close to the case believed there was little point in searching for another culprit. One of those at the game, Joe Bernstein, later reportedly said, 'It was an accident. George did a lot of people a real big favour, though. But it screwed me out of seventy grand.'

There was also a strong suggestion that Rothstein may well have had a point as to the nature of the game in which he lost all that cash. Gambling expert John Scarne recorded in his *Guide to Modern Poker* that Titanic Thompson told him, 'Sure, we [he, Raymond and Bernstein] cheated Rothstein out of the $319,000 in markers, and if it wasn't for that drunk McManus shooting Rothstein we might have collected our money.'

Scarne concluded that, having investigated the incident and spoken to most of the principal participants, he was 'of the firm opinion that McManus, Thompson, Nate Raymond and Bernstein as a team had set out to fleece Rothstein at poker with marked cards and stripper decks.'

VON NEUMANN'S BIG IDEA

BERLIN, 1928

My brain does not have the capacity to benefit from his work, but noted mathematician John Von Neumann, born in Hungary in 1903, who would be deeply involved in the development of both computers and the atomic bomb, once turned his thoughts to poker and published a paper, 'Theory of Parlor Games', on game theory in 1928, while he was teaching at the University of Berlin.

'Real life consists of bluffing, of little tactics of deception, of asking yourself what is the other man going to think I mean to do, and that is what games are about in my theory.'

Von Neumann was fascinated by the psychology of the bluff – although, oddly enough, he was a poor player himself – and in 1944 when his book *A Theory of Games and Economic Behaviour* was published, he concluded that it makes sense to bluff only with the worst hands, rather than indifferent ones.

Von Neumann was endeavouring to capture the intentions and outcomes of successful poker strategy in mathematical terms. The book made an early impact that diminished as celebrated thinkers concluded his reasoning was too narrow to apply to the real world – but poker professionals snapped it up and developed his theories in their play.

Writing about him in May 2006, Tim Harford looked more closely at Von Neumann's theories and concluded that there was an 'ironic' possibility that 'online poker will be dominated by the only poker players able to master Von Neumann's game theory, the computers'.

Top player Chris 'Jesus' Ferguson is believed to be a current devotee of Von Neumann, who was, perhaps, only the second major mathematician to consider poker, having been beaten to the punch by Frenchman Emile Borel. In 1921 Borel published papers on the theory of games in which he analysed the use of poker bluffs and investigated whether the technique could be used in economic and military situations.

A fellow scientist had an apparently contradictory opinion on such matters, and Vannevar Bush (1890–1974), one of the key members of the US atomic bomb development team, wrote in 1945, 'If scientific reasoning were limited to the logical processes of arithmetic, we should not get very far in our understanding of the physical world. One might as well attempt to grasp the game of poker entirely by the use of the mathematics of probability.'

THANATOPSIS PLEASURE AND INSIDE STRAIGHT CLUB

NEW YORK, 1929

Will Cotton's 1929 pastel art work entitled *The Thanatopsis Pleasure and Inside Straight Club*, commissioned by diplomat and novelist Paul Hyde Bonner, is a fascinating caricature-style work capturing one of poker's most notable gatherings in full swing.

The name of the gathering was 'borrowed' from Sinclair Lewis's novel *Main Street*, and 'thanatopsis' means, in loose translation, 'contemplation – or meditation – of – or on – death'.

The Club was originally formed when a number of New York-based literary and journalistic figures met together to play all-night poker sessions. They would play in various apartments and at Nini's French café before they were offered a permanent home in a room of New York's Hotel Algonquin, opened in 1902, on 59 West 44th Street, by owner Frank Case.

'The first game was played at the apartment then jointly occupied by two recently returned members of the 1918 *Stars and Stripes* (the newspaper of the US expeditionary force in World War I) staff, Private Harold W Ross and Private John T Windrich. Sergeant Alexander Woollcott, Heywood Broun and I were at that first game,' recalled celebrated writer Franklin P Adams.

But it was once the group was permanently located at Hotel Algonquin that its reputation grew, enhanced by the fact that Harpo Marx, one of the eponymous Brothers, became a high-profile member and that other luminaries like novelist Paul

Hyde Bonner, Irving Berlin, Jerome Kern, Paul Robeson and Dorothy Parker – the latter attending but rarely if ever playing – were regulars at the gatherings.

'The game itself was usually three rounds of draw, followed by a round of stud – no wild cards and no seven-card games,' recalled Heywood Broun Jr, son of the columnist Heywood Broun.

Harold Ross, another of the driving forces behind the game and the grouping, founded the *New Yorker* magazine in 1925.

Also known more frequently as the Thanatopsis 'Literary' and Inside Straight Club, women were occasionally welcomed into the games with Ross's wife Jane Grant and actress Alice Brady among the more regular female participants – the latter attracting much sympathy for her frequent hefty losses until the other members realised that she was making far more money via her acting career than she could ever have lost at poker.

Alexander Woollcott was said once to have lost $4,000 in one evening, and remarked, 'My doctor says it's bad for my nerves to lose so much.'

Harpo Marx was rumoured to have won $30,000 in one game, but played down the story, saying, 'The most I ever won in a session is a few thousand dollars.' But he seems to have been the most astute gambler of the Marx Brothers – although Groucho is said to have gained that nickname by carrying his poker stakes around in a grouch bag (a small drawstring bag worn around the neck), as well as reportedly having advised promising young actor/comedian Charles Chaplin to 'go into movies' during a poker game at a 'well-appointed whorehouse'.

When the spectacularly bad gambler Chico was asked just how much he had squandered in this way, he replied, 'Ask Harpo how much he's made, and that's how much I've lost.' He wasn't kidding – he once had to write a four-figure cheque to Heywood Broun to settle a poker debt. He warned the recipient not to cash it before noon next day.

Broun later sought Chico out to complain that the cheque had bounced.

'What time did you try to cash it?'

'12.05 p.m.'

'Too late.'

Chico also once declared, 'If I lose today, I can look forward to winning tomorrow, and if I win today, I can expect to lose tomorrow. A sure thing is no fun.'

It was evidently in the genes for the Marx boys, though – mother Minnie was such a keen poker player that she organised regular ladies' games, as a result of which, according to Harpo, 'Minnie's furs and jewels kept shuttling back and forth from the local pawnbroker, since she made a religion of trying to fill a straight.'

But others managed to come out ahead of the Thanatopsis game. 'My father had a good streak in 1921, picking up $1,000 over the course of several sessions,' remembered Heywood Broun Jr. With that money he financed the purchase of a home on 85th Street.

He remembered the club lasting until 1931, 'by which time most of the really big poker players had moved on to [*New York World* editor Herbert Bayard] Swope's House in Sands Point.'

Games at the Algonquin could be lengthy, not for the short of stamina. They would usually get under way after the Round Table – to which most of the poker players belonged – luncheon had finished and would often last through until Monday morning, leaving the players somewhat disorientated on occasion. Franklin P Adams himself was said to have staggered out into the sunlight after a particularly gruelling session where he spotted a young infant in the charge of its governess. Adams shook his head and declared loudly, 'Imagine, keeping a child that age out until this hour!'

Although the group was celebrated for the wit and erudition of its members, the best remembered example of wordplay to emerge during a game was when wealthy businessman Raoul Fleischmann cleaned up with a high-ranking hand and was thereafter referred to as 'Royal Flushman'.

**Alexander Woollcott wrote 'Thanatopsis, A Play in Two Acts', which was never published, but was 'a skit that spoofed the poker games of the Club' and is now part of the Jane Grant Papers collection.

ALICE SPRINGS INTO POKER LEGEND

SOUTH DAKOTA, 1930

Who realised at the time that the frail old woman, nearly eighty years of age, who died in a Rapid City, Sturgis, South Dakota, hospital, on 27 February 1930, was a genuine poker legend?

Alice Ivers was born either on 17 February 1853 in Devon, or in 1851 in Sudbury – but definitely in England in the mid-nineteenth century, the only daughter of a schoolmaster. She was educated in her native land, before moving with her family to Colorado, via Virginia.

She married a mining engineer called Frank Duffield, who taught her to play poker – a game for which it soon became apparent she had an aptitude.

She and her husband settled in Lake City, Colorado in 1875. Gambling was a way of life in mining camps, so Alice and her husband frequently visited the local poker parlours, sitting in on the games.

So, when Frank died in a tragic accident, Alice decided her best chance of making a living might be to become a poker dealer and player. Contemporary reports tell of her 'hanging out' in gambling halls and dealing 'for good money'.

She moved on from Lake City after 1877, and found her way to gambling halls in Alamosa, Central City, Georgetown and Leadville (which in 1879 was a town with 4 banks, 4 churches, 31 restaurants and 118 gambling houses), once breaking the bank at Silver City in New Mexico and then heading to New York to spend her winnings. Her fashionable appearance soon

95

got her noticed, unlike many of the very masculine-looking gambling women of the day. She was very successful – 'I've never seen anyone grow humpbacked carrying away the money they won from me,' she boasted.

In 1891 she was in Arizona dealing poker at a number of gambling dens until a local paper's demand that 'fallen women should be driven from the saloons' convinced her to move on. By this time 'she prided herself on dealing an honest game but could admire crooked work if performed adroitly,' according to an expert reference work on this period, Robert K DeArment's *Knights of the Green Cloth.*

She soon returned to Colorado, though, when she heard about a new mining camp called Creede. Here she managed tables for eight-hour shifts at Bob Ford's – the man who shot Jesse James – Creede Exchange. She had one foible – her religious up-bringing meant she would never play poker or any other gambling game on Sundays, when she got on with her Bible studies. 'I never gamble on Sunday,' was one of her catch phrases. The other, somewhat more threatening, one was 'I'll shoot you in your puss, you cheating bastard.'

She then met and married a gambler called Warren G Tubbs while dealing poker in Deadwood – after, according to some reports, coming to his aid when a disgruntled fellow gambler pulled a knife on him. She shot his assailant.

They wed in 1892 or, according to other reports, in 1899 in Deadwood, or even 1907 – there are quite a few discrepancies in her various life-story accounts!

By now, her poker reputation had spread and she had become a friend of the legendary Calamity Jane (and almost as well known as Bill Hickok's paramour) in the western town of Deadwood, where she played and dealt at Bedrock Tom's saloon. She was universally known as 'Poker Alice'. Deadwood took to Alice so much that she is still represented in their annual 'Days of '76' parade.

She and Tubbs stayed together, later retreating to a chicken farm, until he died in 1910. They seemed to have got on well – if reports that they had four sons and three daughters together are to be believed. He died of pneumonia, in her arms during a blizzard. She drove his frozen corpse on a sled almost fifty miles to Sturgis, where she pawned her wedding ring for $25, which she used to give him a proper burial. That same day she turned up at a Sturgis gambling hall and used her poker skills to win her $25 to claim back her ring.

'At my age,' she was quoted as saying later in her life, 'I suppose I should be knitting, but I would rather play poker with five or six experts than eat.'

Poker Alice had another trademark that must have spread her notoriety – she loved to puff away on an old stogie of a cigar.

Following the demise of Tubbs, Poker Alice moved from Deadwood to Rapid City, and thence to Sturgis. She reverted to type and opened up a gambling venue where, it was said, she was earning up to $6,000 per night, before marrying another gambler – this one called George Huckert. Legend has it that she first took him on as an employee to look after a flock of sheep she had. When his back-wages had built up to $1,008 she apparently declared, 'It will be cheaper to marry him than pay him off.' Huckert soon died; and for the third time Alice was widowed.

In her later years, as her looks vanished, and her clothes sense declined to the point where she was habitually clad in a khaki skirt, a man's shirt and a frayed old hat, she bootlegged booze, ran a house of ill repute in Sturgis, catering to troops stationed at nearby Fort Meade, and took up the odd poker-dealing appointment – notably one at Omaha's Diamond Jubilee.

In 1920 she shot dead a banned, drunken soldier who tried to break in to her gambling house on a Sunday, but she was acquitted by a judge who said, 'I cannot find it in my heart to send a white-haired lady to the penitentiary.'

She spent her final days in a house in Sturgis, subsequently opened to tourists. She became ill and required major surgery with no guarantee of success. Her gambling instinct resurfaced as she told the surgeon, 'Cut away, I've faced big odds before.' This time the odds beat her.

**After her death, and burial in St Aloysius Catholic Cemetery, Sturgis, Poker Alice's reputation began to grow. She is remembered in the name of the Poker Alice Guest House in Sturgis, South Dakota; Nolie Mumey wrote a brief, 500-copy limited edition, 47-page book about her life, *History of a Woman Gambler in the West*, published in 1951 and now highly collectable, selling for around $200. In 1978 Mildred Fielder wrote another book about her – only 24 pages this time, but featuring 16 photographs.

In 1987 Elizabeth Taylor starred in a TV movie called *Poker Alice* that was loosely modelled on our heroine.

Her name also lives on courtesy of highly rated Swiss rock band, Poker Alice, who named themselves after her in 1996, while South Dakota country and western outfit Poker Alice were founded in the mid-80s by lead guitarist Nick Schwebach.

There is also a restaurant in Lake City named Poker Alice Pizza!

POKER BEHIND BARS

CARSON CITY, 1932

The question of how to keep prisoners occupied during their period of incarceration in Carson City, Nevada, exercised the minds of those charged with the job of keeping them content while they did their time.

And they came up with an idea that had not previously occurred to those running any other jails – why not let them play poker? Not only that, why not give them a full choice of casino games to choose from?

Their thinking may have been influenced by the fact that gambling had just been made legal in the state of Nevada and, from that year, legalised and open gambling operated in the National State Penitentiary's 'Bull Pen' – and only ceased in 1967.

This remarkable social experiment was investigated by Dr Felicia Campbell of the University of Nevada, who reported that prisoners told her being allowed to gamble had 'saved their sanity'.

Writer David Spanier described this innovation as 'one of the most extraordinary in the whole history of gambling'.

It was championed by one Jack Fogliani, who was at Carson City for a considerable amount of time – serving from 1953 to 1967 as superintendent and warden. While he was permitting the prison poker and casino games all was calm – there were no reported riots or disturbances.

Those gambling used brass chips to do so, and the prison appointed a cashier who took charge of the money won or lost.

The prisoners built their own casino tables.

Reported the *Sacramento Bee* paper admiringly in 1962, 'Here behind the old limestone walls of the institution two miles east of Carson City, gambling – legal, above board, sanctioned, aided and abetted by prison officials – is high on the list of approved recreations.'

Fascinated by the story, an Italian paper, *Epoca*, reported incredulously to its readers – 'In this prison you can become rich.'

When Fogliani departed, so did the poker playing – the day after Fogliani retired, the new man in charge, Warden Hocker, shut the casino down, replacing it with activities such as knitting.

The prison justified its change of policy at the time by declaring, 'Many beatings and other nefarious activities took place under these conditions.'

'Fogliani seems to have been a very sensitive and sensible warden in his use of the casino to control the prison population. Hocker did not study the function of the casino because he did not have an interest in doing so,' moaned Tomas Martinez, Professor of Criminology at California State University, Fresno. He interviewed an 82-year-old Fogliani, who revealed that there had been gambling at the prison for the best part of a century, much of it taking place even earlier than when the legislation was introduced.

RATS THE WAY TO DO IT

IDAHO, 1933

Superstition is rife among poker players – and one of the most bizarre examples was recorded by an anthropologist, to whom it was described by Native American chief Running Water, from the Bannock tribe, when they met in Idaho's Snake River Desert in 1933.

The anthropologist E Adamson Hoebel was collecting material for his book *Man in the Primitive World* and was presumably not expecting poker to figure in the learned volume.

However, the story related to him by Running Water was so unusual that he felt justified in featuring it as it was told:

A long time ago the Indians around here learned to play poker. I decided I wanted to be able to win at that game, so I went out to seek 'poha' (power).

I went out into the mountains to a place where I knew there were lots of pack rats. I wore only my breechcloth. I ate no food and drank no water.

Continuously I prayed to the pack rats, 'Oh, pack rats! Here I stand, a poor, helpless human being. Take pity on me! Wherever you go, you gather everything in. That's the way I want to be among my people. I want to be able to gather everything in when I play poker.' For three days and nights I fasted and prayed.

On the fourth night a big pack rat, the grandfather of all the pack rats, appeared before me. 'Human being,' he

101

said, 'I have heard your prayers. I am taking pity on you. I shall give you my power.

'Now this is what you must do. When morning comes, scrape up the scale that is formed by our urine on the rocks. Make a small buckskin bag to put it in and wear this always around your neck.

'Now I will teach you four songs. When you want to use my power wash yourself with dry wood ashes to remove all grease and paint. Sing the four songs. Then when you go in to play poker, you will always win. You will be able to gather everything in, even as I do.'

The good news for Running Water, he told Hoebel, was that as he followed these instructions to the letter he began to become a consistent winner at poker.

The bad news, though, he admitted ruefully, was that on one occasion he sat down to play having just taken part in a war dance and not having got round to removing his war paint with dry ashes.

He lost in the game, he became ill, and his poha vanished for good.

Rats!

CHAMP'S KNOCKOUT HAND

MIAMI BEACH, 1935

World heavyweight champion James J Braddock loved a gamble and, while on holiday in Miami Beach in 1935, he teamed up with his friend, gambling expert John Scarne, who devoted his energies to exposing gambling cheats.

Scarne and Braddock were enjoying a day at Hialeah Races when they were approached by some gangsterish-looking hoods, who congratulated the boxer on his recent victory over Max Baer and invited both he and Scarne – who they mistook for Braddock's manager, Joe Gould – for an evening of drinking and poker playing at the Roney Plaza in Miami Beach.

Well aware of Scarne's exceptional card-playing skills, Braddock accepted: 'Jim liked nothing better than to see me sit in at a poker game and deal him the winning hand,' said Scarne.

The pair duly turned up for their evening out. 'We observed that there were in the room three good-looking blondes and three other prosperous-looking men whom Jim and I spotted instantly as shills (players employed by the 'house' to lure others into the game.)'

They had a drink or two before being invited to take part in a poker game already under way in the adjoining suite.

'Jim and I sat opposite each other at the poker table,' recalled Scarne in his 1956 book *The Amazing World of John Scarne*.

The boys started to go to work on us in a hurry. They stacked a couple of hands, palmed cards out of the deck,

103

and signalled each other when to play and when not to play. A blonde was constantly offering us a drink as an excuse to come close and see our poker hands, in order to give signals to the boys. Jim was starting to get impatient and shot me a glance which I knew meant, 'Get going, I'm out a hundred bucks already.' I nodded my head and went to town with the deck of cards.

Those characters never saw so many four of a kinds and full houses in all their poker-playing days. By now Jim was all smiles as he'd got back his hundred bucks and was winning eight hundred dollars of the boys' money.

I had just dealt Jim four aces and one of those characters four kings, and Jim was just scooping in a two hundred dollar pot, when the door opened to admit a portly gentleman named Trigger McGurn, formerly Scarface Al Capone's chief trigger man and then the racket boss of Miami. McGurn was accompanied by two sinister-looking henchmen who were well heeled with automatics. He took one look at the gathering and after flashing a smile and saying hello to the Champ, he turned to the two characters we had met at the race track and, pointing a finger at them he said in a loud voice: 'Out of 20,000 suckers at Hialeah you dopes have to pick out John Scarne to clip in a poker game!'

At that, Braddock chimed in – 'So you mugs thought I was a sucker – the last time that happened was when Maxie Baer signed to fight me thinking I was a sucker for him. I ought to belt you. But why should I? We won a thousand bucks for being taken for suckers.'

**During the same trip, in August 1935, Braddock introduced Scarne, who would build up a reputation as *the* expert on casino and card gambling, to a type of poker neither of them had previously come across.

'Jimmy approached me in the lobby of the [Dempsey Vanderbilt] hotel one night and said, "Professor, I just played in the screwiest poker game ever. It's five-card draw, but listen, the lousiest hand wins over straight flushes, four of a kind, full houses, straights and all the other regular poker winning hands.'"

Scarne couldn't believe it so went to check out the action for himself: 'I was watching for the first time a poker game where the worst hand on the showdown was winning all the pots.'

Scarne and Braddock had just encountered 'Lowball Deuce to Seven', which, wrote Scarne in 1980, 'introduced a new family of countless low poker, lowball and high-low variations of both draw and stud poker'.

FROM C5 TO ACE HIGH

SURREY, 1940

Sir Clive Sinclair will forever be associated with inventing perhaps the single most bizarre conveyance to take to British roads – the Sinclair C5, an eccentric, basically human-powered vehicle which also enlisted the help of a small motor powered by rechargeable batteries. It looked like a mobile sidecar and rendered the user the inevitable butt of stares and remarks when out on the road.

Sir Clive had been more successful in the early 1980s with his ZX80 personal computer, and in 1980 became chairman of British Mensa, the society for the ultra intelligent.

But Sir Clive, born in Surrey in 1940, always had ambitions to make his mark in a completely different field – poker.

And he has managed to do so, appearing in the first three seasons of the Channel 4 TV show *Late Night Poker*, and even creating a bit of a stir in that event when he stormed out 'after blowing £1,500 on the first show' according to the UK Game Show website.

Not all of his poker playing went as badly, though, and he won the first season final of the *Celebrity Poker Club* spin-off event in which he defeated actor Keith Allen.

Sir Clive also saw off a decent-quality field to win the £5,000 first prize in the inaugural UKBetting-sponsored London Poker Night at the L'Equipe Anglais Club – having to play until 2.45 a.m. to claim the honours.

Sir Clive was knighted in 1983 and the Mensa website says of his card-playing passion, 'More recently he has found time to indulge a taste for poker, which he uses as a game of mathematical and social skill to exercise and hone his intelligence.'

CHINESE TAKEAWAY

CHINA, 1940

Oswald Jacoby, a champion bridge player who turned his attentions to poker, told this tale deadpan in his 1940 book *On Poker*:

Then there is the case of the American player in a very high-stake game in China with the help of an interpreter. On the first hand the American picked up the king, queen, jack and ten of diamonds and an odd card. The first player said, 'Ah, foy,' and the interpreter explained, 'He opens the pot for five hundred dollars.'

The American put in five hundred dollars, and the next player said, 'Ah, moy.' 'He raises a thousand,' translated the interpreter. The dealer now said, 'Ah, goy' meaning, the interpreter explained, 'He raises five thousand.'

The betting continued some time with the American always calling. He drew one card; the opener checked, and the American checked without looking at his hand. The next player said, 'Ah, woy,' and the interpreter announced, 'It's a bet of twenty-five thousand dollars.' A couple of players called, and now the American, shuffling his cards thoroughly, spread his hand slowly and saw the deuce of spades. Banging the cards down on the table, he exclaimed, 'Ah, hell!'

One after another, the Chinamen threw their hands away, and the interpreter said, 'Your one-million-dollar bluff won the pot!''

GOING TO WAR ON POKER CHEATS

US ARMY, 1942

John Scarne, the greatest expert on gambling the USA had ever produced, vowed to wage war on the scalpers who were conning the men of the US Army out of their hard-earned pay by cheating them when they played poker and dice.

A few months after the Pearl Harbor attack had brought the Americans into World War II, Scarne found himself given one of the oddest missions ever entrusted by military chiefs – beat the cheats who were preying on the troops' poker and dice games with marked cards and crooked dice. 'My own extension of the underworld grapevine informed me that the card sharps, dice sharks, the common cheaters and hustlers were preparing to do a grandstand business while in the services.'

Scarne had begun his campaign in 1941 by persuading *Life* magazine to run a three-page article focusing on his crusade to fight the cheats: 'Four and a half million copies would be distributed, and the Army's top brass would also read it and, I hoped, would do something about it.'

Scarne was called in by the editors of the troops' army weekly, *Yank*, to talk about what was going on. In order to convince them of his bona fides, Scarne set up one of the strangest hands of poker ever played: he challenged the editors to any gambling game of their choice, and draw poker was selected.

'From a thoroughly shuffled deck, I dealt Colonel Forsberg a full house, Captain Spence a straight, Sergeant McCarthy four kings and to myself the four little aces.'

Impressed with this and other demonstrations, including with dice, the editors told Scarne they would back his campaign. 'A couple of months later Captain Spence called me to advise that he'd received official permission from his superiors, and that I was now to be the only civilian contributor to *Yank*.'

His first article in the paper duly appeared on 12 March 1943. It caused a sensation and as he continued to reveal the ways in which cheats who had joined up were ripping off their colleagues, his reputation came to the attention of J Edgar Hoover, head of the FBI, who wrote to him: 'Your participation in this program is indeed gratifying and I do want to express to you my deepest appreciation.'

Scarne's investigations had already proved to him that 'tens of thousands of decks of marked cards and crooked dice were in use in the armed forces'. He had found his way into a Chicago factory where marked cards were made up and sent out. 'We entered a room in which were seated about thirty girls, each busy with a small camel's hair shading brush and some pens, which they would dip into their inkwells. The girls were busily marking the cards so they could be read from their backs.'

At the factory, Scarne was told of a cheat who had raked in 'fifteen grand in the last three months' and as he travelled home, Scarne was 'fully convinced that tens of thousands of decks of marked cards and crooked dice were in use in the armed forces'.

He visited Camp Mead, Maryland, to check out things at first hand. 'Of the five hundred card games witnessed, which were mostly poker and blackjack, I detected fifty decks of marked cards.'

Through his articles and personal appearances, Scarne began to make inroads. 'As my campaign grew in scope I made a number of overseas short-wave broadcast records for the Army's Morale Division, Armed Forces Radio Broadcast, in which I lectured and answered questions posed by GI letters.'

The *Yank* issue of 23 July 1942 was headlined 'How to spot marked cards in GI poker games'. Scarne also educated GIs about percentages and odds in poker and explained other methods of cheating at poker without marked cards.

As he continued with the campaign so he attracted enemies – anonymous telephone calls threatened his mother. He carried on, nonetheless. 'I visited hundreds of joints which thrived like parasites on the outskirts of Army and Navy bases . . . in the five years of my crusade I was responsible for closing hundreds of these dives.'

Scarne was often assaulted by cheats – 'I received a number of black eyes in altercations' – before 'my luck almost did run out'. He had gone to visit a joint in Georgia where he was advised to make himself scarce, but had the place closed down by army bigwigs.

A week later a car drove straight at him as he was driving home. He swerved and 'as I picked up more speed I was greeted by gunfire and glanced to my right as I heard the crack of shattering glass'.

A shot had pierced the windscreen. Scarne gunned the car up to 90mph and escaped.

Nevertheless, Scarne was convinced it was worth it. 'When I thought of the billions of dollars I had saved 12,000,000 servicemen and women I felt very happy about my five years of crusading. And when I say I saved servicemen billions of dollars, I'm not exaggerating.'

Scarne, who went on to make a film called *You Think It's Luck* in 1952 for the navy, exposing poker cheating methods, was not a modest man, but with due reason – legendary Vegas casino owner Benny Binion was once asked whether he would permit Scarne to gamble at his establishment, and replied, 'I would not let John Scarne gamble at the Horseshoe Casino even if he wore boxing gloves.'

DOING THE DWIGHT THING

WORLD WAR II, 1943

General Dwight D Eisenhower had plenty on his plate with the ongoing problem of helping the Allies win World War II, but GI Simon Davis had heard that the general was not averse to the odd hand of poker, so decided to drop him a line with a request for information, holding out few hopes of receiving a reply.

Davis had written to ask Eisenhower whether he knew the odds of a player being dealt a particular hand. He was so shocked to receive a personal reply that he was happy to have the answer made public.

Eisenhower had written back: 'Although I'm afraid my power of gauging percentages in filling poker hands is a bit overrated, I do like to figure them in my spare time. I haven't had time to go too deeply into the exact figures of your chances of drawing three kings and a pair of jacks – but I'd say they are about 1 in 1,082,900 times. Any mathematician will prove I'm completely wrong, but, anyway, don't count on doing it in a pinch.'

Once his response became public, Eisenhower's popularity soared – and might have helped him become president later on.

Born in 1890, Eisenhower had learned to play poker from an old frontiersman in Abilene, Kansas. He became an excellent player and when he graduated from West Point in 1915 the young 2nd Lieutenant was able to buy his first new uniform from his winnings.

As he moved through the ranks he continued to play – often against a fellow officer, George Patton.

112

But one particular hand of poker had a lasting effect on Eisenhower when he beat a fellow officer who paid him with bonds 'patiently saved by his wife during the years he'd been away to war'.

Eisenhower accepted the payment, but it depressed him and he decided to permit the officer surreptitiously to win the money back. 'This was not achieved easily,' he later admitted, 'One of the hardest things known to man is to make a fellow win in poker who plays as if bent on losing every nickel.'

As a result of this experience, 'I decided I had to quit playing. It was not because I didn't enjoy the excitement of the game but it had become clear that it was no game to play in the army.'

HIROSHIMA – AND PRESIDENTIAL POKER

THE ATLANTIC, 1945

US President Harry Truman revealed to the press corps accompanying him on the cruiser *Augusta*, which was steaming westward across the Atlantic in 1945, the biggest secret of World War II – that the first atom bomb was about to be dropped on Japan. Then he began playing poker with the reporters he had just briefed.

Merriman Smith, White House reporter for the United Press International agency, was there in the game: 'It was just after the Potsdam Conference in 1945. Mr Truman was sorely weary from weeks of high-voltage conferences with Stalin, Churchill and Attlee.'

Also on board was Secretary of State James F Byrnes. 'Talking with Byrnes meant talking business, and for a few days at sea, the president wanted a mental rest.' So, to avoid the discussions, Truman 'played poker morning, noon and night. The stakes were high. The limit was the size of the pot, which frequently zoomed into hundreds of dollars.'

The shipboard games would start as early as 8.30 a.m. and usually ended between 11 p.m. and midnight. 'I was one of three or four members of the press party invited to these sessions,' recalled Smith.

One morning they were called in as usual. 'It turned out not to be poker that morning. The president instead reviewed in great detail the development of the atomic bomb and the forthcoming first drop on Hiroshima. Once this graphic secret was told to us for later publication, out came the cards and chips.'

Looking back, Smith believed, 'Mr Truman was not a true gambler. Poker was his safety valve.'

What's more, Truman was not over-keen on winning. 'Playing with comparatively low-salaried reporters he became quite embarrassed when he won heavily. Consequently he would stay on utterly impossible hands in an effort to plough his winnings back into the game. I know of no one who ever got any state secrets or information from Mr Truman in a poker game, unless it was the chilling fact that aces beat kings.'

Smith again travelled with the president – this time on the White House train – in 1946 when elections were being held 'which swept the Democrats out of control and ushered in the Republican 80th Congress.'

His daughter, Margaret, interrupted a poker game when she brought in a sheaf of telegrams showing some vital results. 'He looked down briefly at the figures, then smiled up at his daughter. "Yes, I see." He quickly returned his attention to the game, and said, "Deal".'

Also in 1946, Winston Churchill travelled on the presidential train en route to Missouri to make a speech, and challenged Truman to a game of poker – which he told him he had enjoyed playing since the Boer War.

Presidential aide Clark Clifford later recalled that 'Churchill was not very good at the game' and after just an hour's play he was some $300 down, whereupon Truman ordered his fellow players to 'not treat him badly'.

'Finally, however,' remembered Clifford, 'as the evening was drawing to a close, we moved in a little on our guests. When the dust had settled and we tallied up Churchill had lost about $250.'

Truman also enjoyed playing poker with friends on the presidential yacht *Williamsburg*, once writing to his wife Bess, 'You know, I'm like a kid; I can hardly wait to start.'

A description of his games at that time described how 'each player started the game with a $500 stack of chips, and if anyone lost it all, he could get a second $500 stack. About ten per cent of every pot was put in a "poverty bowl", which was distributed $100 at a time to players who had lost their second stack. Truman liked an eight-handed game best.'

On 27 July 1955, Truman sat down to write a letter to one J Frank Rope in Kansas City, apparently about a card printed by the Union Pacific Company that explained the order of value for poker hands.

Truman wrote to Rope: 'Eddie [Jacobson, a mutual friend and former Truman business partner] told me you didn't believe this arrangement. It seems that Harriman [one of Truman's war-time negotiators] and the UP are in favour of it. Suppose you bring this card to our next meeting and we'll pass it on. Maybe you'd better consult Eddie about it too.' He signed it 'Harry S Truman'.

In early February 2006, that letter, complete with its original envelope, was up for sale on the abebooks.co.uk website for just under £1,500.

PISSING AWAY A QUARTER OF A MILLION

LAS VEGAS, 1947

Nicholas Dandalos – a.k.a. Nick the Greek – and Joe Bernstein, two of the biggest gamblers of their generation, were facing each other in a winner-take-all $150,000 buy-in five-card stud showdown at the Flamingo Hotel in Las Vegas in 1947.

Bernstein had a pet superstition – maybe for well-founded personal safety reasons, or maybe just so no one could pass behind him to catch a glimpse of his cards – that he would never sit down in a game unless he could do so with his back against the wall. He was well aware of the fact that when Wild Bill Hickok broke that identical habit it ended with him being shot from behind.

Nick the Greek – of whom we will read more later – seemed to harbour no such concerns and alongside him was a beautiful showgirl, his date Marie, who was happy to sit and watch Nick playing his cards.

The game was an hour old and it was going Bernstein's way – he was $25,000 to the good, meaning his stash of chips was now worth $175,000, while Nick was reduced to $125,000.

The current hand was building nicely – there was $90,000 in the pot when the pair received their last upcard. Nick drew an ace, Bernstein was showing a pair of twos.

Nick looked at his hole card. Marie looked, too. Nick 'tapped out' for his remaining $80,000. He shoved his entire stash into the middle of the table. As he did so, Marie pushed

117

her chair back, stood up and announced she was heading to the ladies' room.

Nick made a comment to Bernstein – encouraging him to match the eighty grand if he dared. If he did the hand would be worth a cool quarter of a million dollars to the winner.

Bernstein stared at Nick's ace, jack, six and five, comparing them with his own visible pair of twos. Knowing that his own hole card did not improve his hand, Bernstein had to deduce whether the Greek had a hidden card to match any of the visible four – if he did so then Bernstein knew he could not win.

He thought some more before, slowly, he called the $80,000 bet.

The Greek immediately threw in his hand, commenting, 'You win, Joe. Marie blew the pot for me – you read her actions.'

He was spot on. Bernstein confirmed, as Nick had feared, that he had deduced Marie would have refrained from leaving the room had she believed her boyfriend had a hand good enough to beat Bernstein.

Bernstein was relieved that Marie had decided to relieve herself. The Greek was left pissed off.

In another unfortunate – for him – incident, Nick the Greek was reportedly cheated out of half a million dollars by a scalper wearing swimming trunks with a telescope trained on his victim.

Dandalos was lured into a two-week gambling session of poker and gin rummy at the Flamingo.

He and the cheat who took him for the cash played in their swimwear around the hotel pool. Unknown to Nick at the time, his opponent concealed about his person a tiny radio receiver via which he was supplied with prompts as to the hands Dandalos had been dealt by an accomplice positioned in a hotel room overlooking the pool, equipped with a telescope and state-of-the-art radio transmitting equipment.

As a further aid to cheating, the table and chairs at which the games took place were fastened to the ground so they would stay in sight of the telescope viewer. Nick accepted his massive losses when the game was over, but was eventually acquainted with the truth of the methods by which he had been parted from his cash.

Friends of Nick made it their business to endeavour to reclaim his losses, only to find themselves arrested when the perpetrator accused them of attempted extortion. They were found guilty and sentenced to ten years' imprisonment.

Nick revealed the details of the scam to famous gambling specialist and writer John Scarne when they were together at the Flamingo Hotel Casino bar shortly after the affair had taken place.

Commented Scarne later, 'The cheat met an untimely death when a hidden bomb in his automobile exploded, sending him to kingdom come.'

It is also said that when writer Ian Fleming heard about this incident, he adapted it, and wrote it into his James Bond novel *Goldfinger*.

FLAMINGO PLAYERS DIDN'T HAVE A LEG TO STAND ON

FLAMINGO CASINO, 1947

The Flamingo was one of the most notorious of the Vegas casinos. It was founded and built by the notorious Benjamin 'Bugsy' Siegel, who had pulled together a syndicate not necessarily consisting of entirely conventional or respectable backers to create a state-of-the-art casino-hotel in the previously little-regarded desert town of Las Vegas.

Opened on 26 December 1946 and named for his girlfriend, Siegel was probably already doomed when it launched, thanks to his somewhat unorthodox business practices, which seemed to include helping himself to some of the cash put up by his well-connected backers. Top stars of the day like comic Jimmy Durante, singer Baby Rose Marie and band-leader Xavier Cugat attended and performed at the opening bash, described by one observer as being comparable to 'the gaudy opulence of a top hoodlum's funeral'. Siegel himself was killed by a bullet on 20 June 1947 in Beverley Hills – no one was ever convicted of his murder. Some say he is buried behind the Flamingo.

In hindsight, Siegel was vindicated as the Flamingo overcame its initial difficulties and became a great success, attracting many more lavish casino-hotels to open up alongside it.

But during Siegel's short and eventful heyday, one of the most audacious scams was pulled on the poker game at the Flamingo by a Nevada gambler called Jimmy Altman, who had obviously thought long and hard about how to get an 'edge' over the high-rolling players there.

120

He plotted with three accomplices and they duly put their plan into action.

The Flamingo shop sold playing cards, and one day a stranger wandered in there and bought up their entire stock of playing cards.

Later, Altman arrived and entered the store, attempting to buy a pack of cards, only to be told they were sold out – just the answer he had hoped for.

Altman went to the casino and joined the poker game.

As Altman sat down, staff in the hotel shop were dealing with a customer who had become very upset and abusive when informed that there were no decks of cards available for purchase. The store manager was called. He apologised profusely and promised to get some in stock just as soon as humanly possible.

An hour or so into the poker game, Altman made a point of ostentatiously examining the cards being used. He said nothing, but made sure that his fellow players noticed what he was doing.

Around about this time a man had arrived in the hotel store, asked to see the manager, and produced a business card showing him to be a playing-card salesman new to the area making a call to introduce himself and look for prospective business.

The manager greeted him like the answer to his prayers and asked whether he happened to have any packs of cards with him.

To his relief, the salesman said that he had. The manager bought the lot, blissfully unaware that each of them was marked, in a way with which Jimmy Altman was entirely familiar.

Altman's apparent misgivings about the cards being used in the game had by now begun to register with his fellow players, some of whom were also now convincing themselves that perhaps the reason the cards were not running for them had something to do with the cards, rather than their playing ability.

Altman now spoke about his misgivings and requested they should be allowed to play with a fresh deck – preferably one about which there could be no suspicion at all. Maybe, he suggested, one of the dealers or casino staff might nip to the hotel store and bring back some decks from there with which to continue the game. The other players agreed.

The new cards were duly sent for and introduced to the game – from which Altman then proceeded to extract an estimated one million dollars.

HOW MOSS NICKED THE LONGEST GAME

LAS VEGAS, 1949

Nicholas Andrea Dandalos, who we have met in an earlier story, was born in Crete in 1893. The family sent him to America to seek his fortune at the age of eighteen. He lived in Chicago before moving to Montreal where he became friendly with a leading jockey, Phil Musgrave, whose advice helped him to clock up a half-million dollars of profit in six months.

Back in Chicago, Nick promptly lost all of his winnings at the dice and card tables but set about studying the art of casino gambling to the extent that casinos soon tried to entice him to work for them.

Nick remained on the punter's side of the table and reportedly once won a Los Angeles city block in a game and on another occasion challenged an arrogant opponent to a one-card draw for $550,000 – which was declined.

He was also said to have played a marathon session of faro lasting for ten days and nights, which was ideal training for a stunt that would gain him lasting fame in the poker world.

On a Sunday in January 1949, by which time he was universally known as Nick the Greek, he decided he wanted to take on the best player in poker circles. He approached Vegas casino owner Benny Binion with a proposal, and a match was duly arranged against the legendary Johnny Moss. Moss was at that time in his early forties and would, some 25 years later, become the first person to win three World Series of Poker Championships.

Binion's only stipulation for the game was that it should take place in public view.

Both players agreed and the showdown began. As Moss's biographer Don Jenkins commented, 'Johnny and Nick didn't mind playing for days at a time. Poker was what they lived for. Poker was their life. They got their nourishment from fast action.'

Breaking only to sleep, and playing almost every variation of poker they could come up with, the pair – joined from time to time by other passing high-rollers who wanted a taste of the action and who were charged a minimum buy-in of $10,000 – struggled for supremacy. One dramatic hand saw Moss dealt a nine in the hole with a six showing. Nick was showing an eight. Moss then caught another nine while the Greek received a six. Confidently, Moss raised $25,000.

Johnny drew a two, Nick a four. Johnny bet $30,000. The Greek called.

Johnny's final card was a three, Nick was dealt a jack. He staked $50,000,

Knowing only one card could beat him, Johnny re-raised. The Greek called, putting himself all in. There was $500,000 on the table.

'I guess I have to call because I think I have a jack in the hole,' said Nick.

'If you've got a jack in the hole you're going to win one hell of a pot,' declared Moss, watching intently as the Greek turned over his hole card – a jack.

They battled on for an amazing five months in total, at the end of which period Moss was a reported $2million to the good.

When the Greek lost what was to be the final pot he rose from his chair, bowed slightly to his opponent and uttered the words that would go down in poker lore: 'Mr Moss, I have to let you go.'

Dandalos went straight to bed. He would never hit such heights again, and was eventually reduced to playing in $5 limit poker games in Gardena, California.

Some say he was a great gambler, others a compulsive one,

and writer Carl Sifakis observed wryly, 'The fact is no casino ever refused the Greek's action, which tells a great deal about his true ability.'

Moss recalled the contest in 1975, remembering that hand worth $500,000 – 'the biggest pot of my whole life' – which the Greek won. 'Stud was my worst game. We played about two, three weeks. I beat him outta seventy, eighty thousand. Stayin' up four, five days at a time, sleepin' for twenty hours then playin' again. Then we played draw poker, my best game. I must've beat him outta four hundred thousand. Might've won more. The entire game must've lasted four months, maybe five. And then, when the end comes that ole Greek smiled, got up from the table and he says to me, 'Well, I guess I got to let you go, Mr Moss.' I had broken him. But that Greek was a real gentleman. He just got up and he smiled and he set off to bed.'

SOLO POKER

TEXAS C. 1951

Someone playing a solo hand of poker against himself is not a common sight, but Doyle Brunson remembers an occasion on which it occurred.

It was back in the days when he and the other players in the game were college students, and it happened because of a disagreement between two of the other players – characters known as Scotty and Professor Math. The former was 'strong and temperamental'. The latter, nicknamed because of his ability with figures, would often criticise his fellow players.

They were all taking part in a game of Dealer's Choice, in which after each hand the deal was passed on to a player who could then choose his own form of poker.

When one of the dealers chose seven-card stud with deuces wild, Professor Math declined to take part, claiming that the unpredictable nature of the game negated his mathematical ability.

The others played and the deal moved on again, until it reached Professor Math who nominated 'draw poker, nothing wild', at which point Scotty looked at him and declared, 'Deal me out.' Going round the table in turn, each of the other players refused to take part.

Embarrassed, Professor Math handed the cards to the next player.

Scotty intervened, returning the cards to Professor Math. 'It's your deal,' he said, recalled Brunson, 'so, ludicrously, PM was intimidated into dealing five cards to just himself.

'"You forgot to ante," Scotty reminded. So PM anted. And then Scotty made PM wager right to the end, then show his hand and take his own pot.'

Only then did the game move forward. 'After that, PM played all the hands quietly.'

Brunson used the story to indicate that at the poker table 'you don't need only poker skills – you need public relations skills, too. You can't always have things your own way.'

POKERGATE?

EN ROUTE TO THE WHITE HOUSE, 1952

Richard Nixon is perhaps best remembered for the Watergate scandal that brought him down from the presidency in 1974 and which suggested that maybe his word was not always to be regarded as wholly accurate.

So, having announced in 1952 that he was giving up playing poker, maybe some suspected he would eventually take up the cards in anger again somewhere down the line.

Nixon, born in California in 1913 to a mother who wanted him to become a Quaker missionary, was an unlikely candidate to take up poker in the first place. Not only did he do so once he joined the navy (later writing in his autobiography, 'I learned that the people who have the cards are usually the ones who talk the least and the softest; those who are bluffing tend to talk loudly and give themselves away'), but he earned a reputation as the best player in the service and was said to have won between six and ten thousand dollars doing it – which he used to finance his campaign in 1946 for Congress.

He apparently took up the game while in the Solomon Islands, where fellow officer James Stewart would later recall: 'He said to me, "Do you think that there's any sure way to win [at poker]?" And I said, "Well, if you don't think you have the best hand going in, get out. Drop. Don't ante up." I said, "The trouble with that is that you'll probably drop three or four hands out of five and it's very boring and I haven't got the patience to do it." Well, to our intense surprise, he did exactly that. And he won . . . more frequently than he lost and he sent home to California a fair amount of money, I have no idea exactly how much, but my estimate was between $6,000 and $7,000.'

Another naval man who served with Nixon, James Udall, said, 'Nick was as good a poker player as, if not better than, anyone we had ever seen. He played a quiet game, but wasn't afraid of taking chances. Sometimes the stakes were pretty big, but Nick had daring and a flair for knowing what to do.'

He certainly became keen on the game – website classroomhelp.com reports, 'He became such a dedicated player that he once turned down a chance to have dinner with Charles Lindbergh when it conflicted with a game.'

Nixon himself later said of his poker talent: 'I believe my ability in the field is somewhat exaggerated,' but admitted, 'I was fairly successful playing poker overseas.'

In 1952, Nixon became running mate to presidential candidate Dwight Eisenhower – also a poker man – ending up as vice president and calling time on his poker exploits. Well, almost – he later confessed to relapsing and playing again, but only once, and, besides, he 'just broke even', so presumably barely regarded that as even playing.

Not everyone is convinced about Nixon's poker abilities and the former world champion Amarillo Slim boasted in his 2003 memoirs, 'I've played poker with presidents – Lyndon Johnson and Richard Nixon,' adding of the latter, 'I played with Nixon before Watergate at a private club in Washington, and he wasn't as tricky as advertised.'

HUGHES CLEANS UP

LAS VEGAS, C. 1953

Howard Hughes became a major player in Las Vegas in the mid-60s and early 70s. At one time he owned half a dozen major casinos – including the Desert Inn, his favourite, where he had taken up residence in a suite of rooms in 1966, only to discover that the management wanted him out as they had promised the accommodation to high-rollers and visitors.

Never a man to let a small matter of this nature come between him and his requirements, the flamboyant millionaire promptly bought the Desert Inn for a cool $13.25m in order that he could continue staying there.

He then became interested in buying up other hotels and casinos and had acquired several more, including the Landmark, before the government stepped in, fearful that he may single-handedly take over the resort for himself.

Hughes had first visited Vegas in the 40s and 50s and was reportedly an inveterate gambler at the tables, albeit there are few reports of him playing poker.

However, he did enjoy watching the game being played and in around 1953 he became friendly with the great Johnny Moss.

In his biography *Champion of Champions*, written by Don Jenkins, Moss told of how Hughes appeared at the Flamingo casino and took a close interest in the game in which he was taking part. Hughes was rebuffed by a number of players before 'Johnny told him that he could sit behind him. Hughes sat there for several hours,' with Moss showing him the hands he was playing, reported Jenkins.

Hughes began to show up regularly when Moss was playing and the pair became friendly. During one game, Moss happened to remark that he had heard of a high-stakes poker game in Birmingham (USA) that he would have liked to frequent, but had not been able to find a convenient way to fly there.

'Hughes overheard the remark and called Johnny aside. He offered the use of one of his private planes: "I don't care how long you stay, but feed my pilots while they're there, and find them a place to sleep."'

Johnny flew out to the game, but on his return found himself called upon to intervene in a situation involving Hughes that would require as much subtlety as he would expend on a cagey poker hand.

Staff at the Flamingo told Moss that Hughes's personal hygiene – or lack thereof – was causing a problem. The eccentric rarely washed, but hotel staff didn't dare risk coming straight out and raising the subject for fear that he would take, firstly, umbrage and, secondly, his high-rolling gambling business elsewhere.

Moss accepted the challenge. 'Standing beside him one day, Johnny sniffed the air, and looked Hughes directly in the eye: "You know, something smells bad. I think one of us is going to have to take a bath. One of us has b.o. – and I just got out of the shower."'

Subtle as a brick, you may think – but apparently effective, as Hughes duly departed, only to return smelling somewhat more fragrant, albeit still clad in the same clothes.

Hughes was very impressed with Moss and one day remarked to Johnny that he couldn't believe how much money he made at the game.

'This is my business,' Johnny replied. 'How much money do you make in your business?'

131

DO NOT ADJUST YOUR SEX

LOS ANGELES, 1954

When 31 poker-playing women were surveyed in 1954 in an effort to determine how well adjusted they would turn out to be compared with their non-poker-playing equivalents, the assumption was they would come off second best.

Psychologist W H McGlothlin studied female players, chosen at random, using clubs in Gardena, twelve miles south of Los Angeles. The survey included within it the Bell Adjustment inventory, which would yield scores on home, social, job, health and emotional adjustment. Their scores would then be compared with the norms for the general population.

Gambling psychologist Michael B Walker predicted, 'One might expect that the better adjusted women would stay within traditional female roles and that only socially deviant women would frequent the poker clubs on a regular basis.' So he was surprised at McGlothlin's results as he 'found that the poker players were significantly better adjusted than the general population on the social, emotional and home adjustment scales'.

Explaining further, McGlothlin declared, 'If playing poker can be classified as a hobby, it is quite possible that it may contribute to good adjustment by combating boredom. In our society, many middle-aged women find that time weighs heavily on their hands, and the resulting boredom is often a contributing factor to conflicts in various facets of their lives. To the extent that the game of poker offers a stimulating activity to occupy the participant's time and interest, it may well be an adjustive factor.'

PUTTING ON THE RITZ

LONDON, 1954

John Aspinall was one of the most flamboyant figures on the London gambling scene in the 1960s when his Clermont Club became enormously popular with a certain circle of society, among whom was one Lord Lucan.

Aspinall sold the club in 1972, in order to 'spend the rest of his life with animals', according to his biography. He founded an extraordinary zoo at Howletts, a grand but decaying house in Kent, and was forced into the gambling world to raise money as the costs of his animal antics increased.

But it was poker that first brought him into the world of gambling. When he was at Oxford University he met up with a friend from the marines, Desmond Dunphy, who organised poker sessions at his rooms.

Aspinall watched closely – he 'witnessed ten whole games with careful attention before he decided he would attempt to play, and from that moment, with the cards in his hand, he knew that he had found his metier,' wrote Brian Masters in *The Passion of John Aspinall*.

Aspinall began to clean out the low-stake games at Oxford, and engineered himself an invitation to a rather richer affair, organised by Ian Maxwell-Scott, great-great-grandson of Sir Walter Scott.

Maxwell-Scott played poker for the 'almost sensual pleasure' in placing bets, but Aspinall was more pragmatic and he preyed on the game, which 'was distinguished by very high stakes and very poor players'.

Aspinall raised his sights again and became involved in a regular game, which attracted artists and wealthy hangers-on. 'Aspers' soon dominated this game, too. 'He seemed possessed of a unique microscope to look into the soul of his opponent and understand his psychology. He knew what card a man would play before he had decided to play it, because he knew his temperament and character.'

His style included a love of drawing to an inside straight and an instinctive understanding of when and how to bluff, which 'earned him a glamorous reputation'. He also, declared Masters admiringly, 'used his will in order to win'.

Such was his personal charm, though, that many of his victims apparently felt positively grateful to be able to lose to him!

By this time, though, Aspinall was partial to gambling in other ways, too – it was 'poker in the morning, the races in the afternoon, dog racing in the evening and perhaps another card game until late at night'.

Once out of Oxford, Aspinall had to begin to make his way in the real world and poker became less important to him, although in 1954 he ran a poker game at the world-famous Ritz Hotel.

Not that the Ritz either knew or permitted it. He and Maxwell-Scott managed to stay at the hotel for seven months in Room 505 in which 'they ran a small game of husband-and-wife poker, the takings from which enabled them to pay their bills'. They pulled the same stroke at the Park Lane Hotel.

As the room became an early, illegal betting shop, also being used for the placing of horseracing wagers, so the management of the Ritz eventually cottoned on to what was going on and demanded full settlement of their bill, which was beyond them, despite almost landing a betting coup on a horse – which won the race, only to be disqualified.

Aspinall by now had realised it was more profitable being a bookie than a punter and played less and less himself as the casinos he ran became more lavish and profitable.

He died in the year 2000 after a lengthy battle against cancer, and his biographer believes, in my opinion not completely accurately, that 'in years to come, no one will remember Aspinall the gambler – his renown as a visionary zoo-keeper will be assured'.

Care to bet on that?

HOW 'JAMES BOND' LEARNED AN EXPENSIVE POKER LESSON

BERKSHIRE, 1957

Ian Fleming won worldwide fame as the creator of the immortal, archetypal Cold War spy James '007' Bond. Bond was a frequent visitor to casinos where he would gamble confidently.

Fleming also enjoyed a gamble, but after 1957 he was always very wary of playing poker.

That was the year in which he penned the piece that would become the introduction to the critically acclaimed 1958 book by Herbert Yardley, *The Education of a Poker Player.*

Fleming began his article by complaining that playing poker for money – 'a legal game over half the world' – was illegal in the UK, and pointing out that a London club, the Hamilton, had been fined £500 in a 1945 show trial on the grounds that poker was not a game of skill. This was a decision with which Fleming did not agree – calling it 'hypocritical balderdash'.

Fleming then praised the book, which he said he had bought when it was originally published in America. He tried to persuade his publisher, Jonathan Cape, to bring it out in Britain but they declined – until Fleming offered to write a preface for it.

'I am not a good poker player,' confessed Fleming. 'Poker is a cold-hearted, deadly game that breaks and bankrupts men,' he admitted.

Then he revealed, 'The last time I played poker I lost more than I could afford in rich brassy company in a house at Sunningdale.'

His fellow players introduced variations of the game which Fleming was 'mocked' for not understanding. Finally, 'numb with martinis and false bonhomie', he pretended he could play a poker variation called Minnie Everley: 'I remember the name but not the variation.'

In his confusion and embarrassment Fleming 'played a ragged, brash game that cost me dear. I was fleeced and deserved to be.'

Fleming asserted that had he at that time read Yardley's book he might not have been taken in so easily. 'Very few fine card players are the sort of people you and I would like to play with,' he warned his readers before concluding that, 'not as a poker player, but as a writer of thrillers, I can recommend this book to every consenting adult card player in Great Britain'.

**In 2006 Fleming's *Casino Royale* was the latest James Bond movie, starring new actor, Daniel Craig. The film featured poker rather than the baccarat which had appeared in the original novel, to cash in on the current popularity of the game.

POKER COMES OUT

ENGLAND, 1960

During the 1940s, prosecutions of poker clubs for being unlawful became commonplace in England – to the extent where at one point, respected QC Mr Gilbert Beyfus argued during a case that if the prosecution were successful, the only lawful card game in England would be snap!

Despite this, he lost that and other cases as poker and, by implication, virtually every other card game was deemed unlawful.

The confusion had arisen because of the country's archaic laws, the most recent of which dated from 1854 and laid down that any game which was not a game of 'mere skill' must be considered unlawful.

For some while poker and bridge in particular had been given the benefit of the doubt, but in the 40s suddenly there was a series of prosecutions. 'It was claimed that the Acts (from 1854 and 45) meant that any game that was not of undiluted skill was unlawful, and clearly the deal and the draw introduced some element of chance into poker,' explained Terence Reese, who appeared as an expert witness on poker's side in some cases, in his 1962 book *Poker: Game of Skill*.

A 1941 ruling was crucial in establishing a precedent and in finding against the legality of poker, when Mr Justice Croom Johnson observed: 'Whether or not there is largely an element of skill in the game of poker or whether there is largely an element of bluff in it I do not know, but I am quite certain that the predominant element in it, lawful or unlawful, pleasurable

138

or not, is that of betting on one's hand and hoping that the other fellow has not anything so good as one's own, or that one can bluff him out of holding on to the game until such time as the showdown comes and one produces one's own hand when the other man asks to see it. All that is done on the basis that the game is largely one of backing the value of the cards which the chance of the deal has put into one's hand.'

The enforcement of the law was somewhat inconsistent. 'The police, we may assume, were often preoccupied with crimes even more harmful to the community than playing cards,' observed Reese somewhat wryly.

Eventually, as 'poker seemed to occupy an uneasy position somewhere in no-man's land', it began to be played again in clubs, 'albeit somewhat nervously'.

But even in 1950, in George Coffin's book *The Poker Game Complete*, he quoted a British lawyer as saying, 'English law as it at present stands is a bitter and unwavering enemy of poker, and that those who use premises for the playing of poker do so at their peril.' He added, emphatically, 'The law is the law and poker remains illegal – at least until any findings of the Royal Commission to the contrary are announced and implemented.'

Then the Betting and Gaming Act of 1960 defined 'gaming' as playing for money any game in which there is any element of chance. But under the new code neither gaming nor the keeping of a place for habitual gaming was unlawful in itself, subject to certain rules.

Poker could not be played in pubs and bars – even though dominoes and cribbage could – but it was allowed in a private room on premises used as a club.

**As this book went to press the precise legality of poker played in clubs and other 'public' places was still somewhat unclear.

FAMOUS FIVE

TEXAS, C. 1960

Five Texan poker players – Jack Straus from Houston, Jesse Alto from Corpus Christi, San Antonio's Tom Moore, Pinky Rhoden from Lubbock and fellow Texan 'Ducky' Mallard – have been credited with, if not actually creating, then certainly popularising the game of Texas Hold 'em while they were on the road trying to avoid the draconian US laws that pretty much prohibited poker playing anywhere other than California and Nevada.

Setting up games quietly and surreptitiously to avoid both the law, who would break the games up for being illegal, and the bad guys, who would break them up to steal the money, the five staged high-stakes games all over cattle country – even disguising what was going on by pretending they were staging religious conventions or meetings of fraternal organisations.

The game they played was no-limit hold 'em, and this variation soon became known as the 'Cadillac of Poker' as it arrived in Vegas.

Those days are long gone, you might say – yet the American authorities are still doing their darnedest today to prevent their citizens from playing poker – online, at least, claiming it is illegal – despite strenuous efforts from interested parties to prove otherwise.

THE GUY THEY LOVE TO HATE

WISCONSIN, 1964

How many other players would be so proud to be dubbed 'everyone's favourite guy to love to hate' by a top magazine, that they would feature the quote on their own personal website?

The man who in 1989, became the youngest world champion ever, that's who – Phil Hellmuth Jr, who was born on 16 July 1964 in Wisconsin.

And that is not the only critical public comment to be aimed at Hellmuth, who 'has proven himself to be one of the most proficient tournament poker players of all time and one of the most cantankerous poker figures of all,' according to buypokerchips.com, which also believed that 'fans love to root against' him.

Writer Allyn Jaffrey Shulman described one of the reasons why: 'You might see his 6ft 5in body dramatically sprawled out on the floor of a World Poker Tour TV set, kicking his feet and bemoaning a bad beat like a child having a temper tantrum.' He did just that in Atlantic City when, after unexpectedly losing a hand, he promptly threw himself to the floor.

Hellmuth defends himself by saying, 'If I play poker for 50 hours you'll love me for 49 of those hours. When I lose it I look like a jerk – until I see one of my friends laughing at me.'

By 2005 Hellmuth had become the top WSOP money-winner of all time and had collected nine gold bracelets. Online encyclopaedia Wikipedia commented, 'While his WSOP bracelets bring him much recognition, his notoriety is likely more due to his perceived inability to handle adversity and accept defeat gracefully.' The latter trait was demonstrated when he stormed away from a table where he had lost, declaring, 'I guess if luck wasn't involved I'd win every one.'

He explained his own background, telling an interviewer, 'I am originally from Madison, Wisconsin. I found a poker game while I was a student at the University of Wisconsin – I guess I never stopped playing poker after that.'

Having been successful in Wisconsin, Phil took a big reality check when he played for the first time in Vegas. He joined a game in the Dunes poker room, and sat down next to *Kojak* actor Telly Savalas. The game lasted for 72 hours straight off. He lost heavily – and did so on his first ten Vegas trips, wiping out a bank of $20,000.

He went back to Wisconsin to regroup and recover some cash.

His entry to the big time was sealed on Easter Sunday 1988 when he won a tournament at the Reno Hilton.

Not short of confidence, Hellmuth believes with typical modesty, 'Most poker players consider me the number one poker tournament player in the world.' He explains, 'What makes me great is my ability to read people. I think my greatest strength is that I have no one particular style.'

This may help to explain the title of his autobiography – *Poker Brat*.

Hellmuth himself has predicted that he could earn 'anywhere up to $400m off the poker table' and he helped in this direction when he teamed up with Oakley eyewear – who call him a 'poker icon' – to develop his signature series of poker-style sunglasses. He also gave his name to a cellphone game.

But someone must like Hellmuth – he is married to Kathy, a doctor, with two children (one named Phillip III) and his several poker books have been bestsellers.

Hellmuth is not a man to wager against lightly – even if he is not in his preferred environment at a poker table. At the beach, relaxing one day, he and fellow player Huck Seed disagreed over how long a man could stand in ocean water for.

Hellmuth put up $50,000 to say that Seed would be unable

to stand up to his shoulders in ocean water for eighteen hours.

Seed took the bet – but had to give up the ghost after just three hours, then having to paddle back to the shore shamefaced and much poorer.

But for all his controversial image, one poker expert reckons the answer to countering him is obvious: 'Poker at its highest level is about exploiting the weaknesses of your opponents,' wrote Les McMullen in late 2005. 'Instead of complaining about Phil, other players should be using his flaws against him.'

NO KIDDING, STEVE, YOU'RE A LOSER

SILVER SCREEN, 1965

Steve McQueen lost perhaps the most famous poker hand ever – in the 1965 film *The Cincinnati Kid*, based on the 1963 book by Richard Jessup, and ever since arguments have raged among poker purists as to the authenticity of the hand, and the way in which it was played out.

Writer and poker player David Spanier called the showdown 'a somewhat incredible hand of five-card stud, illustrating the interaction between courage and restraint'.

And the way Spanier read the eventual defeat for the Kid was that he 'allowed his calculation of the chances to be overridden midway through the hand by overconfidence'.

Fellow author Anthony Holden said, 'The film blows itself away with a climax still laughed to scorn in card rooms the world over', yet despite that it cemented McQueen's thespian reputation to the extent that in 2005 he posthumously topped an Internet survey designed to reveal the 'Favourite Poker Playing Character', beating Paul Newman – for his roles in *The Sting* and *Cool Hand Luke* – into second place.

McQueen, playing the Kid, comes up against Lancey 'The Man' Howard, played by Edward G Robinson. In the movie, the Kid draws a full house of aces and tens against Howard's queen-high straight diamond flush. Complains Holden, perhaps overlooking the fact that it is supposed to be entertainment, 'The chances that both of these hands will appear in one deal of two-handed five-card stud have been

144

calculated at a laughable 332,220,508,619–1.'

In fact, so outlandish is the nature of this showdown, many critics argue that any player beaten in such a manner would immediately be suspicious. As *Poker Player* newspaper writer Michael Weisenberg wondered, 'Why didn't the Kid start screaming foul? If YOU got beat like that, would you just walk away shaking your head, muttering to yourself, "Well, them's the breaks?" I doubt it.'

However, others point to the fact that to arrange a fix of this nature would be just too blatant and surely anyone organising such a scam would make it less obvious – perhaps letting one player have a slightly higher but not outrageous hand. 'By all means enjoy the movie,' adds Weisenberg, 'so long as you pretend it's three sevens being beaten by three nines.'

Holden believed the showdown would have been improved had the Man won by bluffing the Kid into folding a superior hand. Writer Phil Gordon just thinks the Kid was the victim of 'the greatest bad beat in the history of poker cinema'.

But not everyone is so critical. Rustin Thompson of moviemaker.com believes 'the tension-wracked final hand is worth watching again and again for a crash course in how to bluff and when to bet. When Robinson is scolded for making what appears to be a reckless raise, he sums up the game's timeless, intractable appeal: "It gets down to what it's all about – making the wrong move at the right time."'

Long-time pro Roy Cooke summed the arguments up well: 'If you put any of the world's top players in either the Kid's chair or the Man's, they might play this hand under these rules and these circumstances just this way. I'm not saying they would, but they might. I wouldn't – but that might be why I'm not the Man!'

By the way, if you reckon a poker fan is kidding when they tell you they have read *The Cincinnati Kid*, win yourself a few bob by asking them what the Kid's Christian name is – they will be hard pressed to come up with the correct answer, which is . . . Eric.

145

NOT SUCH A HAPPY CHRISTMAS

LOS ANGELES, 1966

Nick 'the Greek' Dandalos, born in 1892, died in Los Angeles on 25 December 1966. Some $500m in gambling stakes had passed through his hands, and he would, posthumously in 1979, become one of the founding members of the Poker Hall of Fame along with world champion Johnny Moss.

By the time he died he had fallen on hard times, despite in his heyday having played for some of the highest poker stakes ever recorded. Indeed, in his *Gambling Secrets of Nick the Greek*, author Ted Thackrey Jr claims that 'Nick lost the biggest single pot in the history of poker – $605,000 – to [fellow gambler Arnold] Rothstein.'

Nick, said Thackrey, declared, 'I came out $70,000 ahead of the game. I'd taken Arnold for $675,000 during seven hours of play leading up to that one bet.' The next day, Rothstein apparently sent Nick a brand-new Rolls-Royce as a token of his esteem, but he returned it. 'Who needs a car in New York?' he asked.

Despite having been reduced to playing in small-time games in the final stages of his life, it was said that Las Vegas casino owners provided him with a 'tab' in order to bring crowds into their premises, attracted by the prospect of watching Nick play or, indeed, playing against him.

Nick did not believe in taking life too seriously, whether his fortunes were waxing or waning, and once memorably took eminent scientist and brainbox Albert Einstein on a tour of Las Vegas casinos, when that worthy was director of the Institute for Advanced Study at Princeton, New Jersey.

Einstein was fascinated by his experience, and more than a little amused when Nick introduced him to gamblers who had no idea of his celebrity as 'Little Al from Princeton – controls a lot of the action around Jersey'.

He was said to have donated $5m to charitable causes and philanthropically shelled out the college fees for 29 children of friends and much more anonymously by settling the hospital bills of friends.

And he would earn a unique tribute from professional blackjack player and writer Jacques Black who, in 1993, said of him: 'For me, Dandalos resembles a Shakespearean hero, imbued with many virtues – courage, dignity and humility – yet ultimately brought to grief by one fatal flaw. That flaw was that he desired action above all else.'

Nick the Greek was laid to rest in Las Vegas, transported in a golden Cadillac, in a ceremony paid for by casino owners. Writer Harry Mark Petras, who attended, calling it 'a funeral befitting a king,' adding, 'Maybe generals and kings gambled for bigger stakes when they put armies and kingdoms to war, but no man risked higher wagers at a table than Nick.'

FROM SCHOOL DROPOUT TO
TRIPLE WORLD CHAMP

NEW YORK, 1967

Stu Ungar dropped out of school on New York's Lower East Side in 1967, aged just fourteen – to become a professional gambler.

He was still a professional gambler – and a three-time world poker champion – when he was found dead aged 45 on 22 November 1998 in a motel room on the Las Vegas Strip.

Within weeks of turning pro in his early teens, Ungar had won $10,000 playing gin rummy – only to blow the stash at the Aqueduct racetrack.

He had become a much-respected gin rummy pro before, fleeing a bookie to whom he owed a substantial sum, he arrived in Las Vegas in 1978 and began to take a serious interest in poker.

His baby-faced appearance rapidly earned him the nickname of 'The Kid'. He was rarely to be seen without his trademark round, blue-tinted glasses. After being introduced to cocaine in 1974, it wasn't long before he became an addict.

Having won the world championship at Binion's Horseshoe Casino for the first time in 1980, aged 26, becoming the youngest winner, he repeated the feat the very next year. He won the Super Bowl of Poker three times, along with many other major tournaments. But in 1997 he had to be bankrolled to enter the world championship – yet he won again.

By now, many rated him the greatest poker player ever and this triumph, which followed a spell in the wilderness, prompted him to pledge, 'I decided to wake up. No one has ever beaten me playing cards. I have only beaten myself.'

But he squandered his $1m winning purse within two months and started to fail to turn up to tournaments. He was reportedly back on drugs.

Ungar's biographer Mike Sexton said of him, 'He had a genius IQ and a photographic memory. His talent at card games was truly incredible. In no-limit hold 'em he was relentless. Describing how Ungar played no-limit poker is like talking about someone who is a fearless warrior with a combination of the artistry of Mozart, the moves of Michael Jordan and the focus of Tiger Woods.'

Some of Ungar's success could be attributed to his single-mindedness at the table. 'Away from the table I'm really not that bad a guy. But when the cards are dealt I just want to destroy people.'

That single-mindedness came at a cost. He was unworldly. 'He did not understand much about anything except poker,' said casino owner Bob Stupak. 'Stu would not know how to pay an electricity bill. I don't even know if he had a driver's licence.'

Licence or no, he did once own a car that was wrecked when he failed to top it up with oil. 'Why the hell didn't they tell me you had to put oil in the car?' he asked plaintively.

He was as bad a golfer as driver – and once lost $80,000 on his way to the first tee, on the putting green. 'I would estimate that Ungar lost several million dollars playing golf,' said Mike Sexton.

Stupak arranged a deal to bankroll Ungar for the 1998 world championship. He gave him some spending money, which Ungar took before checking in at the Oasis Motel. Two days later he was dead – a mixture of narcotics and painkillers reportedly triggered the heart condition that killed him. There was $800 in his pocket – apparently all the money he owned in the world.

Daughter Stefanie poignantly recalled Ungar refusing an invitation to the White House. 'What would I talk to the president [Clinton] about? We have nothing in common,' he told her.

JIM FIXED IT

WEST VIRGINIA, 1967

Jim Boyd discovered he had what it takes to become a poker player at the age of sixteen.

The West Virginian's father was the owner of a nightclub that functioned downstairs, while the family apartments were upstairs. Dad had booked a 'semi-famous singer' named Ronny Dove to perform at the club.

Ronny was a gambler and, with twenty minutes between sets, he wanted to gamble. So Ronny and Jim's dad set up a game of no-limit five-card stud upstairs on the kitchen table, with Ronny trying to win more than his fee and Dad trying to recoup the fee.

'The place was packed and my dad had to leave to break up a fight,' recalled Jim.

'Here, son, play this hand for me,' his father told the teenager.

'I bet with an ace in the hole and a queen up, and Ronny called. On the end he caught a king and bet $700, everything he had in front of him. I thought and thought, and right about the time that I said, "I call" my father walked back into the room.

'"What are you doing?" he yelled.

'Looking confidently at me, Ronny said, "King."

'I asked, "How many?"

'He answered, "King!"

'And I scooped in the pot with my ace high. Right there and then I knew that I had an instinct for poker.'

150

Jim was right, and in 1989 he took up the game full time after losing his job.

With two young boys to support it was a bold move, but he headed for the WSOP and made himself $40,000 – only to fall into the mistake made by so many good poker players – losing the lot at other gambling opportunities like horses and craps.

He turned things around and finally landed a big win in Vegas, enabling him to build the family a home.

He won a big tournament at Foxwoods – which landed him with the nickname Mr Foxwoods – until he acquired another when he won $13,000, slipped back to just $40, then built it up again to win $40,000. After this he was dubbed 'The Comeback Kid'.

Boyd continued to survive on the circuit and became a popular player, summing up his philosophy: 'If I can make a nice living and get back home to West Virginia for the summer to do a little fishing and barbecue some hard-shell crabs in the backyard with my family, I'm happy.'

WORLD CHAMPIONSHIP

BINION'S HORSESHOE CASINO, LAS VEGAS, 1970

Lester 'Benny' Binion was the man who unleashed the World Series of Poker – now justifiably described by Doyle Brunson as 'the granddaddy of the poker tournaments' – onto an unsuspecting world back in 1970.

Actually, Tom Morehead (also reported as Moore) of the Riverside Casino (other reports say the Holiday Hotel) in Reno had first come up with the idea in 1968, when it was dubbed the 'Texas Gamblers' Convention' and involved stud, draw, lowball and hold 'em and produced, by vote, a 'King of Cards', who was awarded a silver cup. For its first two years, Johnny Moss won and retained the cup, but, rather like the way certain record companies turned down the Beatles in their early day, so Morehead allowed Binion to take the concept forward, eventually creating the most prestigious and wealthiest contest in poker. Ironically, at the time Binion began staging the event, poker was not normally played in his casino.

Binion, who survived pneumonia-related health scares in his Texan childhood years and therefore managed to avoid the stress of ever attending school, had been a booze bootlegger and craps-game organiser. He was found guilty of first-degree murder in 1931, and shot and killed another man five years later – self-defence, this time. He arrived in Vegas in 1946 where, according to writer Andy Bellin, he carelessly 'lost about $400,000 playing poker'. Nonetheless, he kept going, and eventually opened his Horseshoe Casino there in 1951 –

attracting tourists in by displaying $1m in a horseshoe-shaped glass container.

He made a point of giving his visitors a taste of the high life. 'If you want to get rich, make little people feel like big people,' was his motto.

In 1953 he was imprisoned for four and a half years for tax evasion and forced to sell his interests in the casino, although he remained closely associated with it as a 'consultant'.

Binion, born in Texas in 1904, was buried during the Christmas holidays in 1989, and fellow casino supremo Steve Wynn paid him a thoughtful tribute: 'He was either the toughest gentleman or the gentlest tough I ever met.'

THE NAKED TRUTH

PLAYBOY, 1972

Strip poker is many a man's dream game. The thought of persuading a probably naive and innocent female companion to take part in a game that is very likely to leave her in a state of undress has an undeniable appeal to most males.

The rules of strip poker have always been vague, tending to rely on just how much the male members – sorry, participants – of the game could get away with.

But in 1972 Edwin Silberstang took it upon himself to come up with some hard-and-fast guidelines for playing the game, devoting a chapter of his *Playboy's Book of Games* to the subject.

'Alternate sexes at the table' was a fairly straightforward rule, before he counselled:

> Play draw poker, not stud. Both five- and seven-card stud (where five and seven bets are made respectively) would leave most of the players stark naked after a few hands. In draw, you stand to lose only three articles of clothing if you stay in a game.
>
> Only bona-fide articles of clothing constitute bets. This includes shoes but not band-aids, eyeglasses, jewelry, bobby pins, wigs, false teeth, hearing aids, false eyelashes, fake fingernails and false noses. Outer garments must be removed before undergarments.
>
> No player may withdraw from the game unless agreeing to remove all of his or her clothing.
>
> The game ends when: all the players are naked; half the

players are naked – this calls for a vote as to whether everyone should strip and end the game; the game has gone on too long and the majority of the players vote to strip and end the game.

What you play after the game is up to you.

Author Carl Sifakis in his comprehensive *Encyclopaedia of Gambling* observed, 'There are those who insist that strip poker is the highest-stakes game in cards.' He explained, 'After the draw all players expose their hands and the worst poker hand of all is required to remove an article of clothing,' and he then outlined just two basic rules: '1. Play in mixed company; 2. Play during a heat wave.'

Australian authorities banned 'Strip Poker' computer games in 1995.

In June 2000 a TV game show called *Strip Poker* was screened by the USA Network to a less than positive response. As one Internet critic pointed out, 'Because this is American cable TV, viewers never actually see any nudity.'

Another reviewer seemed to be missing out on the main object of the exercise by complaining that 'most contestants, especially the women, tended to have no knowledge of poker – you could regularly see people losing the game because they gave away cards that were useless to them but extremely useful to their opponents.'

Considering that most viewers would be watching only to see a little flesh displayed you'd imagine the worse the play the better for viewing figures!

In January 2005, strip poker for cellphones was introduced in the States by New York-based wireless-game provider Thumb Play, although website zdnet.com described it unenthusiastically as 'tepid' and another review sniffed, 'about as racy as a lingerie ad'.

Then in August 2005 came another development on the theme as pokernews.com website reported that National Lampoon 'has entered the poker world in its own unique way'.

And that way, it transpired, was 'National Lampoon's Strip Poker pay-per-view specials', which 'have taken two of the world's favourite pastimes, sex and poker, and made a potent mix of hilarity and super-sexy poker action that both teaches the game, albeit for horny newbies, and provides viewers with some of the world's most beautiful eye candy.'

The series was filmed at Jamaica's Hedonism II nudist resort, which would seem to defeat the object of the exercise of strip poker somewhat. 'Each episode,' it was claimed, 'features six female supermodels battling to become grand champion and leave the loser butt naked, with only their smiles left to draw attention away from their toned bodies.'

Variations on the game of strip poker are plentiful and Rustin Thompson of moviemaker.com, who was compiling an article about poker movies, confessed that he had found a fascinating one when he wrote in October 2005, 'Finally, I came upon the web link for Lesbian Strip Poker Pictures. I'd still be surfing that one if it wasn't for the lure of the large fee I'll receive for writing this article.'

Perhaps the most expensive game of strip poker ever played is the one depicted in *The Card Players*, a painting by Colombian artist Fernando Botero, which was sold recently for £1.2m. Disgraced British politician and author Jeffrey Archer said of the work, which is one of his favourites, 'It shows two men and a woman playing cards – the woman is naked, so I imagine they're all playing strip poker.'

A plan by a Vegas club to introduce poker games in which the dealers were (female) dancers who would remove a piece of clothing every time the blinds went up was rejected in early 2006 by the Nevada Gaming Commission.

FIRST FLUSH

MANHATTAN, 1975

'The Players' is an actors' club founded over one hundred years ago by Edwin Booth, based at Manhattan's Gramercy Park. Poker writer Dale Armstrong was a regular there, who enjoyed over half a century of poker playing. On 14 June 1975, Armstrong was dealt his first ever royal flush in hearts there.

'Consider the odds against being dealt one royal flush,' he later wrote. 'Most players never get one.'

So Armstrong was surprised when, less than two years later, on 11 January 1977 and again at The Players, he was dealt another royal flush in hearts.

Then, within a month, on 8 February, fellow player A J Pocock was dealt his first diamond royal flush, followed by another on 1 March.

As a student of the game and its statistics, Armstrong was staggered: 'Not only three royal flushes in as many months, but two to the same player in succeeding months. The odds have to be, literally, more than a billion to one against this phenomenon.'

Poker guru John Scarne calculates the chance of being dealt a royal flush in five straight cards as 649,740–1.

IVEY LEAGUE

CALIFORNIA, 1976

On 1 February 1976 a boy named Phil was born in Riverside, California. The Ivey family moved just three months later to New Jersey and by the time he was eight he was being given lessons in how to cheat at poker by his grandfather, who was doing so 'in an attempt to teach the young Phil a lesson about the dangers of gambling,' according to Ivey's official website.

The youngster may have become aware of the dangers, but that didn't stop him wanting to become a poker player and gambler – because as soon as he became a teenager he was boasting that he was going to become a pro. When he was just sixteen he sat in on an adult game of poker, being hosted by a friend's father. Ivey was the big winner.

When he was eighteen the man who would become known, not entirely to his own approval, as the 'Tiger Woods of poker' acquired fake ID (in the name of Jerome Graham, with which he became so strongly identified that he became known as No Home Jerome) and began frequenting the poker rooms of Atlantic City. To begin with he lost more than he won.

By 2000 he had made two final tables at the WSOP and in 2002 he moved to Long Beach, California, winning three WSOP bracelets at three different games.

By 2005, the man with the trademark basketball jersey (he supports the LA Lakers) had five bracelets and was declaring 'I want to win thirty' when asked if he could overtake the current record of ten, held by Brunson and Chan.

Despite his discomfort at the 'Tiger Woods' nickname (and

he definitely looks a little like the maestro of the tees), Ivey has been known to gamble substantial sums on his own limited golfing ability.

In late November 2005, Ivey won two back-to-back tournaments in Monte Carlo, collecting $1m in the Monte Carlo Millions and, 24 hours later, $600,000 more in the FullTiltPoker.Net Invitational Live.

Inside Edge journalist Alun Bowden, who watched this double triumph, was in no doubt – 'Phil Ivey really IS a poker god,' he wrote of the man who seems equally at home in tournament play or big-money cash games and who believes, 'If you're not a live-game player, you're not a player.'

Another poker journalist, Shirley Rosario, says of Ivey, 'Phil is known to some as the Tiger Woods of poker, but I have to disagree. He is the Phil Ivery of poker, totally in a class by himself.'

ELVIS CASHES IN HIS CHIPS

GRACELAND, 1977

Elvis Presley died on 16 August 1977. The man who found him dead at his Graceland home, 'Diamond Joe' Esposito, met the world's most famous rock'n'roller in the army, became his best man and was a pallbearer at his funeral. And he played poker with 'the King' who, of course, was permanently associated with Las Vegas thanks to his huge hit, 'Viva Las Vegas'.

Esposito appeared on TV's *Larry King Live* in August 2002, explaining to the host how Elvis stayed in the Aladdin Hotel when he wed Priscilla in Vegas in 1967. Esposito recalled how they left Elvis's Vegas suite to play poker in the early hours of the morning: 'We used to go down at four or five in the morning just to play cards in the casino when it wasn't as crowded. But then, all of a sudden, it got crowded, bothered him, and we had to go back upstairs.'

There are many other links between Presley and poker. In August 2005, to great fanfare, the USAopoly company announced excitedly the unveiling of 'the new Elvis "Viva Las Vegas" Collector's Poker Set'.

John M Davis, president of USAopoly, could barely contain his enthusiasm: 'Poker has this country all shook up. Putting a Las Vegas Elvis twist on a classic game like poker is a natural fit,' he declared.

Anything but vulgar or tacky, of course, the promotional material for this desirable item explained: 'What makes the Elvis "Viva Las Vegas" Poker Set so different is the inspiration behind the cool white case. It's designed to look like the famous

160

jumpsuits Elvis wore during his legendary Vegas performances.'

What's more, 'the beautiful red velvet interior holds 200 red, purple and white eight-gram clay chips embossed with Elvis's signature and two decks of high-quality Elvis-themed playing cards. Of course, each of the kings in each of the four suits has been transformed into Elvis performing in concert in Las Vegas.'

You want one now, don't you? And if you do, then you'll also be desperate to track down 'Elvis the Game', a board game which features – wait for it – twenty Elvis Gold Album discs 'that look like poker chips'.

GRIMM'S MONSTER FAIRY TALE

ABILENE, 1978

'Cadillac' Jack Grimm, from Abilene, Texas, just might be the strangest man ever to play poker, according to his biography, when he took part in the 1978 WSOP championship.

If you doubt that description, produce another poker player who 'recently financed an expedition to Scotland to find the Loch Ness Monster and now possesses photographs which he says support his belief in its existence'.

Or one who in 1976 'organised an expedition along the Rio Grande to find the much publicised Big Bird, with its 15ft wingspan'. Apparently, although he and his companions did not sight the creature itself they 'did get to observe some rare whooping cranes'.

Not content with these unusual – for a poker player – trips, Grimm has also travelled to Mount Ararat, 'in search of Noah's Ark'. He came back with what he claimed to be 45,000-year-old wood.

A search for Big Foot was said at the time to be Cadillac Jack's 'loftiest goal – next to winning the WSOP'. He didn't win.

Grimm, a geology graduate from the University of Oklahoma, who maintained that 'drilling for oil in the US, Canada and Australia is a bigger, tougher gamble than poker', was a successful amateur poker player, 'who plays like a pro and provides formidable competition for everyone'. Particularly adept at Hold 'em, he said, 'I play strictly for pleasure, relaxation and fellowship.'

162

In the early 1980s Grimm took part in three major expeditions hunting for the site of the wreck of the *Titanic* – coming, as it transpired, very close indeed to locating the ship and earning the place in history for which he was clearly aiming.

HOW DOYLE KEPT HIS HEAD TO WIN A MILLION

LAS VEGAS, 1978

Doyle Brunson certainly managed to irritate the hell out of his fellow pros in 1978 by the simple expedient of writing a book revealing many – too many for others on the lucrative circuit – of the tricks of the trade.

Well, I suppose Brunson figured, what the hell, I'm already loaded, as evidenced by the title of his instant bestseller *How I Made Over $1,000,000 Playing Poker.* And that volume is still in demand today – a first edition, leather(ette)-bound copy was up for sale for £650 on a book-selling site in spring 2006.

Although the book probably did make it slightly trickier for the elite to continue to fleece the lesser players, there are relatively few players with the necessary willpower to turn a gamble into a calculated investment, so it is unlikely that the flow of mug punters was significantly reduced.

Born in 1933, Brunson was drafted by the Minneapolis Lakers basketball team, only to suffer a knee injury that resulted in him needing a crutch. He graduated from college with a Master's degree in Education, but 'once I accepted the fact that my career in sports was over, I started playing poker to support myself'.

Having exhausted the supply of willing victims on the college scene, Brunson graduated to the Texas underground poker circuit, moving from the small games into the higher-rolling, private games on the north side of Fort Worth – 'the toughest place in the world to play poker. Thieves, robbers and killings were commonplace.'

Brunson held his nerve to contest big-money games held on what was known as the Bloodthirsty Highway. 'Needless to say,' he admits, 'I took a few scratches along the way.' Back then, during the 1950s, one-dollar ante games were the big ones. 'You could make a few hundred dollars a night if you knew what you were doing.'

Brunson did know what he was doing, and began winning consistently, meeting up with like-minded players like Sailor Roberts and Amarillo Slim – 'we kind of watched out for each other'. This mutual watching was important, perhaps a lifesaver. 'To start with you had to keep from getting cheated in the games. You also had to worry about collecting the money if you won. Then finally – you had to keep from getting hijacked.'

Robbery was routine. At one game 'a guy stormed in with a gun and shot a guy sitting right next to me at the table. I remember the guy's head falling off and splattering against the wall.'

Brunson learned the poker player's code of honour – but even that had its limits. At one Austin game, a group of bad guys – seriously bad guys – broke up the proceedings and began to rob the players, demanding to know who was running the game. One of them quizzed Brunson. 'I'm not a snitch, so I answered, "I don't know".' The man whacked him in the belly with his gun.

He was asked again. Still he professed ignorance – and took a smack around the head with a double-barrelled shotgun for his pains. Then the robber cocked his gun, aiming it between Brunson's eyes. 'I'm going to ask you one last time – who runs this poker game?'

'The guy right over there in the green shirt!'

Brunson was learning about life and about how to play poker. 'There were no computers, so I did all the strategy work manually. I dealt out a hand here. I put another hand there. I just kept doing it, thousands and thousands of times, over and over. It got to where I was a lot more advanced in this game than most people.'

So much more advanced, that he won the WSOP in 1976 and 1977, both times with the same hand – a full house of tens and twos, which became known as 'a Doyle Brunson'.

'If I had a mentor,' said Brunson, as he moved into his eighth decade, still playing at the very top, 'it was Johnny Moss, a great player in his day. When he was fifty I thought he was the best player I'd ever seen. And then he reached seventy and eighty, and he lost it. I sure don't want that to happen to me.'

Not everyone has been impressed by Brunson's success. 'My college – Hardin-Simmons University – won't put me in its Hall of Fame because I'm a professional gambler.'

POKER BLAZE

LAS VEGAS, 1980

Poker players, hotel staff and casino gamblers were killed as over eighty perished and some eight hundred were injured in a horrific fire at the old MGM Grand (not to be confused with the current complex of that name) Hotel and Casino on 21 November 1980.

The hotel had opened in December 1973 and had over 2,000 rooms. The fire started in a restaurant and spread rapidly through the building.

The *Las Vegas Review-Journal* (www.reviewjournal.com) carried a story in November 2005 suggesting that one of the pit bosses on duty that day 'received a call from a higher-up with a hush-hush request. He and a fellow pit boss were told to go to the back of the still-smoking hotel and retrieve as much currency and high-number poker chips as possible from the cashier cage.'

The story alleged that they carried out seven or eight large plastic trash cans, full of money and chips, wading through water up to their hips.

'Based on what we knew they kept in the cage, we estimated we took out $7 to $8million. Where it went, I'll never know,' the website's source was quoted as saying.

The story ended: 'The next day, he said, it was reported that most of the hotel's money had burned in the fire.'

HOLY HOLD 'EM

VIRGINIA, 1983

Perhaps the most bizarre book about poker was given a Virginian birth, appropriately enough, when in 1983 attorney Richard Davis came up with the inspired – some might say blasphemous – notion that the best source of advice for the game of hold 'em poker was none other than the Holy Bible.

And lo, the *Hold 'em Poker Bible* was created, and was warmly welcomed: 'The finest book ever written on hold 'em,' enthused Poker Hall of Fame member Bill Boyd, while Howard Schwartz, owner of the Gambler's Book Club, declared, 'It's sacrilegious for a hold 'em poker player to be without the *Poker Bible*.'

In his introduction to the book, which did indeed feature a 'Ten Hold 'em Commandments' section, Davis was at pains to explain why the term 'Bible' was appropriate – one of its definitions, according to *Webster's New Collegiate Dictionary*, is 'a publication that is pre-eminent in authoritativeness'.

And Davis had certainly done his Bible studies, taking as his theme for the opening sermon, sorry, 'Introduction' to the book, his belief that 'The Holy Bible has good advice for all regardless of your religious persuasion or non-persuasion.' To illustrate he quotes Proverbs 10:4: 'He becometh poor that dealeth with a slack hand: but the hand of the diligent maketh rich.'

You must admit, he has a point.

Davis, who served for five years in the USAF, came up with dozens of appropriate biblical quotations with which to make his case, and among his hold 'em Commandments are: 'First – The first thing thou must consider is position. If it and thy cards are poor, then to play will make thee poor also,' and 'Tenth – Thou must keep an even temperament. Without composure, frustrating circumstances will cause thee to play less than thy best.'

Davis's book boasts a jet-black cover with gold-embossed letters apparently spelling out 'Holy Bible', until a closer look reveals that the Y of Holy actually consists of a capital letter D, the word Poker as the stem of the Y and the word 'em also as part of the cunning design.

STAMPING OUT CHEATING

CALIFORNIA, 1984

Darwin Ortiz has been called America's leading authority on crooked gambling.

Fortunately, Ortiz, who is capable of dealing you a hand of four kings and himself four aces, is one of the good guys, and has done his best to alert the rest of the world to the methods of the bad guys.

Ortiz published his book *Gambling Scams* in 1984, identifying a host of ways in which both amateur and professional cheats have been known to take their victims to the cleaners on the green baize of the poker table.

He related the cautionary tale of a card-sharp friend of his from South California, who, having popped out one afternoon to mail some letters and replenish his supply of stamps, decided to visit a nearby Gardena poker room to deal himself some spending money.

He picked out a lowball game, in which players attempt to win by playing the lowest possible hand, and which seemed to harbour some promising victims, and joined in.

Making his preparations for the 'sting' he palmed the four of hearts, slipping it into his pocket for later use.

A while later he was dealt a two, three, five, seven and king. Now was the moment to switch the king for his four, leaving him with an unbeatable hand. He made his move and bet the limit, confident that he could not lose.

'Without another glance he placed his cards down and continued to push up the pot at every opportunity,' reported Ortiz.

By the time the showdown arrived there was a decent amount to be won and the hustler duly spread his hand face up for all to see as he reached for his ill-gotten gains.

However, there for all to see, stuck to the front of the four of hearts, was a US postage stamp, which had obviously attached itself to the card while it was in his pocket waiting to be introduced into the hand.

There was a tense silence, finally broken by an elderly lady who was looking incredulously at the card. 'So,' she said, 'somebody mailed you a four of hearts?'

Ortiz firmly believes in the principle of 'once a cheat, always a cheat'. He writes of a college friend 'who paid all his tuition from the money he won cheating at fraternity poker games. He later attended one of the most prestigious law schools in the country.' Ortiz is convinced that, however well off his law practice has made him, 'he is [still] taking every opportunity to cheat his well-to-do friends at cards.

'He is just that kind of guy.'

Triple world champion, Johnny Moss – who once discovered a doctor in Brownsville, Texas was running a scam by tampering with a table leg so he could remove and replace cards on the table at will – had his own view of cheats: 'When someone steals from a game they are stealing from the best player, because the best player will eventually end up with the money.'

Of course, there is always a different take on every story and those doing the cheating at poker must, by definition, be very quick thinking just in case they should be discovered and, certainly back in the days of the Wild West, shot dead. And the tale is told of the Dodge City card sharper who thought he was being suspected of cheating, so he quickly ordered a sandwich – into which he palmed the hidden cards he had been using – and ate the evidence.

A Tombstone poker cheat from those days, Dick Clark, used a huge diamond ring that he wore as a 'shiner' or mirror, enabling him to monitor cards as they were dealt – others used polished cuff links or gold watches to get an edge. Other crooked players were said to have sandpapered the ends of their

171

fingers, thus making them more sensitive to lightly marked cards.

It is said that in the Wild West, cards were dealt to the left during poker games, so that a man could easily reach for his gun with his right hand if he suspected cheating was going on.

Not too many left-handed poker players about, then!

YOU'RE TELLING ME

USA, 1984

Mike Caro's Book of Tells, subtitled 'The Body Language of Poker', was published in 1984 and suddenly everyone was examining their opponents across the green baize for giveaway signs that might indicate whether they were bluffing or double bluffing.

'Caro's book explains how to read the people you are playing against,' said top gambling writer Frank Scoblete, who rated the publication of the book the 67th most significant twentieth-century gambling event in his top one hundred, calling it: 'A seminal work on the human side of poker.'

It meant that twitches, habits and involuntary movements were being analysed and interpreted – but also helped very shrewd bluffers to wrong-foot their opponents by deliberately pretending to have telltale indicators that were actually nothing of the sort!

'Tell(s)' is now a well-recognised poker term, with gambling author Richard W Munchkin defining it neatly: 'A habit or mannerism that gives away information about a player's hand', while Trevor Sippets, in his 2005 book *Poker,* explained further: 'A million years of social interaction has endowed human beings with a wide range of subconscious gestures and mannerisms . . . The ability to spot these gestures and comprehend their meaning will enhance your prospects at the poker table and an awareness of their presence might help you gain control over some of your own involuntary movements.'

Tells were, of course, around before Caro drew attention to

173

them, but he was the first to give them the honour of an entire volume based on their cause and effect, even though author Dale Armstrong had observed in 1977, 'Tells are what the professionals depend on for their livelihood and survival.'

Armstrong recalled a player who always 'paused to light his pipe when he had a good hand' and another who would drum his fingers impatiently as he waited to play decent cards.

One player who became convinced that his Adam's apple would involuntarily twitch when he had a good hand took to wearing a scarf at the table. Many other players now wear sunglasses, hoods and hats in an effort to keep their tics to themselves.

Website poker.about.com came up with an interesting 'tell' theory: 'Often, inexperienced players will hold their breath if they are bluffing.' I think you might be able to check that theory out – when the player keels over through lack of oxygen!

'Some of the top players in the game will stare at the vein on the top-side of your face for blood-pressure changes,' warns website www.playwinningpoker.com's article on tells, adding that during a big hand 'you may see the chest expanding abnormally, or you may notice the player's voice become slightly higher as he makes a comment'.

Respected poker writer and TV presenter Phil Gordon feels, 'Experience is probably your best ally against physical tells, as your hand probably won't be trembling – generally a sure sign of a monster hand – after the four or five- thousandth time you've bet into the river.'

You might imagine there would be no truck with tells for online poker players, but not everyone agrees. A website called billrini.com featuring 'Bill's Poker Blog' advises, 'Many players will tell you that online poker tells either don't exist or are difficult to judge. That's a load.' He goes on to explain the tells, but one just might detect quite how serious he is when the first one features a computer image of a player with something emerging from the sides of his head: 'Notice the smoke coming out of the player's ears?' asks Bill. 'That's a dead giveaway.'

It certainly is. And it might be possible if the idea from Internet 'blogger' 'flipchipro' caught on: 'Let me be the first to propose that the next generation of online casino poker incorporates a web-cam aimed at each player that transmits your live mug shot to the opponent's screen where it can be used to read your tells.'

In 1980 the bearded Caro, born in 1944 and known as 'Mad Genius', invented a poker-playing computer called ORAC. Flamboyant gambler Bob Stupak took it on in a $500,000 heads-up match, which saw man beat machine. In that year, renowned gambling authority John Scarne said of the man he called 'Crazy Mike' that 'in my opinion (he) is one of the five best Five-Card-Draw Poker players in the world'.

But before Caro, a poker writer called R F Foster was on to tells, albeit describing them as 'mannerisms', in his 1922 *Practical Poker*: 'I knew a player once who had a habit of pulling his ear with his right hand when he had very good hands.' The player was eventually alerted to his tell and, to stop himself doing it 'he used to separate his cards, holding two or three in one hand and the rest in the other hand, so that his hands were both occupied and he could not caress his ear'.

Problem solved? Earily enough, no. 'Had he done this with every hand, it would have been all right, but it was only when he felt the temptation coming on to pull his ear that he separated his cards; so whenever he held his cards that way we used to pass out immediately, unless we could beat three aces.'

In a 1947 advice book *Win at Poker* the authors passed on a 'tells' story during a game involving three men and a dog playing poker together. A man entering the room looked at the scene and could hardly believe his eyes. 'That certainly is a remarkably clever dog,' he said.

'I don't think he's so clever,' replied one of the players. 'Every time he gets a good hand he wags his tail.'

MATTER OF PRINCIPLE

US SUPREME COURT, 1985

When the US Internal Revenue Service decided to relieve gambler Billy Baxter of $180,000 of his poker tournament winnings on the grounds that poker should be regarded as a game of luck, and therefore winnings should be subject to the same tax requirements as lotteries and sweepstakes, he was unimpressed.

So much so that he launched a suit against the US government, arguing that poker should, in fact, be considered to be a game of skill and therefore only subject to the same deductions as any other earned income.

The first hearing, in a federal court in Reno, Nevada, saw the judge rule in Baxter's favour, telling government lawyers, 'If you think poker is luck, I invite your side to play Mr Baxter in a poker game.'

The government appealed and the case was heard again, this time in the Eighth Circuit Court of Appeals in Los Angeles, where the judge also found for Baxter.

The case ended up in the US Supreme Court, only for the government to drop the appeal without taking it in front of the highest court in the land.

The IRS duly returned Baxter his $180,000, which barely covered his legal fees.

'But of course that was never the point. It was a matter of principle,' declared Baxter.

Baxter learned to play poker in Augusta, Georgia in the late 50s, initially supporting the learning procedure with winnings he made from pool. Soon, he became good enough at poker to earn himself a tidy living, winning seven WSOP bracelets along the way.

DEVILFISH

HULL, 1986

David Ulliott was a successful poker player long before it became trendy – in 1986 he invested some of the winnings he had been making into a gold and diamond-cum-pawnbrokers shop in Hull.

At that time his reputation had not spread much further than Hull, but in 1997 he was playing at the Four Queens casino in downtown Vegas against a group of Chinese players, who were so impressed by him when he cleaned them out that they gave him a nickname which was to stick with him permanently.

They likened his technique to a small, dangerous resident of the South China Sea, a fish that can be eaten, but unless prepared very carefully by an experienced chef may do you potentially fatal damage as a result of the poison it carries with it.

It is the Devilfish, a.k.a. *Inimicus Sinensis*. Or perhaps not. A little fish-based research suggests that I.S. is the 'official' name for the 'Spotted Ghoul' from the Stonefish family and that the Devilfish is the Inimicus Diductylus aka Chinese Stinger. Birmingham-based poker promoter Stephen Au Yeung is credited with bestowing the nickname in Des Wilson's 2006 biography, 'Swimming with the Devilfish'.

Ulliott had beaten a player called Men 'The Master' Nguyen during that Vegas stint and the next day a newspaper ran a headline saying 'Devilfish devours the Master', much to Ulliott's delight.

He was so taken with the new name that he had a pair of

178

double-finger jewel-encrusted 'rings' struck bearing it, which he still wears today. And as his reputation has grown so has his following – you can now purchase a Devilfish nodding doll for $3, should you be so inclined.

Nor is the Devilfish much less spikey than his aquatic namesake. 'Intimidation is a big part of poker,' he says. 'I sit down at a table and most of the other players instantly create a shepherd's pie in their trousers.'

His aggressive playing style has also been known to create tension with other players. He once asked a player puffing on a large Montecristo: 'Is that right? If you've got a small cock you smoke a big cigar?'

FIND THE LADY

GERMANY, 1987

German police reported during 1987 that a Cologne punter had lost the ultimate stake during a poker hand – his wife!

The man had then taken the winning player home with him to collect his dues, only for the unenthusiastic spouse to grab their baby, flee the house and call the cops. 'He wasn't charged, but he had a lot of explaining to do,' said an admirably understated police spokesman.

Two years later, in May 1989, Rio de Janeiro police were called in when Brazilian Pedro Becone lost at poker, as the 31-year-old had been playing for similarly high stakes – his wife, Maria.

Despite actually being on honeymoon at the time, Pedro had left his 29-year-old bride alone in bed while he went out to play poker and enjoy a drink or two. However, he overdid the boozing and, after a drunken game of poker with local man Joe Cortez, Becone offered 'the services' of his wife as settlement for his losses.

LITTLE WHITE LIE?

CHICAGO, 1988

It was reported in 1988 that when seventeen-year-old David White decided to stop playing once he had won $100 from his mother Lemira during a poker game in Chicago, she became so angry that she pulled out a gun and shot her son dead.

Lemira later told police, 'He was cheating, anyway.'

Another poker dispute from the same year ended in one of the players pointing the finger at his opponent. Steve Grove called Bill Smith a cheat as the pair played poker at Evesham in Worcester. The dispute turned into a brawl, during which Smith bit off Grove's finger.

NOW, REMIND ME AGAIN . . .

CALIFORNIA, 1991

After 106 years it was announced during 1991 that California was lifting its lengthy ban on the game of stud-horse poker.

The only trouble was, it seems nobody could remember just how it was played. The game was apparently outlawed back in 1885 – for reasons also now lost in the mists of time.

The only clue to the game seemed to lie in an old tale that it had been invented by a certain 'Poker' McCool who reportedly lost his favourite stallion while playing it.

Previously, in March 1947, the attorney general of California had been called upon to make a distinction between stud-horse poker and stud poker. He controversially ruled that the two were the same. But, given that there has never been any definition of stud-horse under the law, that seems unlikely.

So, the mystery remains – but if you believe you know how to play stud-horse poker, please let us know.

ARCHIE EDUCATES PROS

LAS VEGAS, 1992–3

What may well have indeed been what top gambling writer Frank Scoblete called 'one of the greatest runs in Vegas history' saw Greek immigrant Archie Karas turn a $10,000 debt into a $17m asset at the poker tables during 1992 and 1993.

Karas (real name Anargyros Karabourniotis), an immigrant to America at the age of seventeen, started his working life as a waiter in Los Angeles where he began hustling for money at pool. He also learned poker and cost himself his job by cleaning out the restaurant owner.

As his gambling increased he won and lost huge sums and by December 1992 reckoned he had managed to get through $2m in high-stakes card games, and was left with just fifty bucks in his pocket when he drove into Vegas.

Making for the Mirage he talked a fellow gambler into loaning him $10,000 to 'take a shot at the biggest action in the card room' in a high-staked razz (a seven-card stud variation) game. He quickly won twenty thousand and paid off his debt.

From there Karas took on a big-shot hotel executive at pool for $10,000 and more per game – beating him out of between $1m and $2m.

Now the pool gave way to poker, at which the businessman was rated highly – not highly enough, though, and in early 1993, after a week of heads-up, Archie beat him for $1m.

He then put out an all-comers invitation to high-rolling poker players to take him on.

Chip Reese was the first to take the bait, and they met in

April 1993 at Binion's Horseshoe where the games of choice were razz and seven-card stud. In a fortnight Karas was a reported $2,022,000 ahead of the game.

Finding it difficult to get the poker action he wanted – 'Nobody would play poker with me for that much' – Karas turned to the craps tables, winning and losing seven-figure sums, and at one time had all of the Horseshoe's $5,000 chocolate-coloured chips in his possession.

At last another poker challenger turned up – Stu Ungar. Karas again came out on top, winning a reported $900,000 in a six-hour showdown, at which point those who had been bankrolling 'The Kid' cried enough. 'The nearly $1m loss hurt more than Stuey's pride. It made those people who had still been willing to back him gun shy,' wrote Ungar's biographers, Nolan Dalla and Peter Alson.

Doyle Brunson came and had a go at Karas. They broke even, but Karas claimed, 'He didn't want to play high enough.'

Puggy Pearson and Johnny Chan took him on, and Chan managed to beat him – once out of four attempts.

At the end of what became known as 'The Run', Karas was said to have 'busted' fifteen of the world's top players and at the peak of his winning streak been $17m ahead of the game.

'I've gambled more money than anyone in the history of the planet. I don't think anyone will ever gamble more than I have. I'm the biggest ever,' boasted Karas, who is still around today playing the tournament circuit.

And few argued. But how much of that $17m – some reports suggested it was even more than that – remained in his possession for how long is another question. One source alleged, 'The only thing he bought out of that money was a car. He lost it all in poker games.'

TIPPED OVER THE EDGE BY POKER

WASHINGTON, 1994

Speaker of the House and respected Democrat Tip O'Neill, who died in 1994 aged 81, was an inveterate poker player throughout his lengthy political career.

Born in 1912 and growing up in Cambridge, Massachusetts, 'he developed a lifelong love for baseball, betting, cards and common folk,' wrote Byron Liggett.

O'Neill started to take poker seriously at high school and college, and would play under the local baseball bleachers 'to keep his father from discovering he was gambling,' according to one biographer.

He graduated from Boston College in 1936 and ran success-fully for the state legislature. When he won he gave much of the credit to his poker-playing friends, 'because without their hard work I never would have been elected'.

In 1952 O'Neill won a seat in the House of Representatives, which had been vacated by one John F Kennedy, and again poker came to his aid: 'Poker provided me with a great oppor-tunity to meet my fellow legislators, which in turn enhanced my political career' – not a sentence one could ever anticipate reading in connection with a British politician.

'When I went to Washington I played cards probably every night of the week,' admitted O'Neill. At the University Club where he played, seven-card stud, and variations thereof, was the game of choice, with raises limited to three. He could win up to $400 on a good night, taking it from representatives and senators, Democrats and Republicans. 'There were no parties or factions in that room. There was only good fellowship,' remembered Tip, although some of the losers may not have put it in quite that way.

In the late 60s O'Neill, who had become a Democratic leader in Congress, became critical of the president, Lyndon Johnson, over the war in Vietnam. In his book *Man of the House*, O'Neill revealed that one of his most momentous and far-reaching decisions over Vietnam had begun over a discussion in a poker game in which General David Shoup was playing.

Shoup had recently resigned as commander of the Marine Corps because of his disagreement with the administration's war policy. O'Neill came to the same conclusion and he became one of the first members of Congress to oppose Johnson over the issue.

O'Neill never disguised his love of poker, and believed that 'poker and politics require some of the same skills. In each case you need to understand the people you're playing with as well as how to calculate the odds . . . It helps enormously if you know when to bet, when to fold and when to sit tight.'

He did come up against perhaps the most highly rated poker-playing president, Richard Nixon, who was once complaining to O'Neill about his lack of luck in a poker game. 'You know, I'm sick and tired of reading what a good poker player you are,' replied Tip. 'As a matter of fact, you're one of the worst poker players I've ever seen.'

O'Neill was hailed by Senate Republican leader Bob Dole as 'one of the great political leaders of our time' following his death – and, poker writer Byron Liggett added, 'one of the nation's most important poker players'.

LAUGHING HIS HEAD OFF

MERSEYSIDE, 1994

Council worker John Font was so pleased when he was dealt a winning poker hand that he almost literally laughed his head off, it was reported in 1994.

The 32-year-old Merseysider was so excited when he saw the full house he'd been given that he threw back his head to roar with delight – and the pressure split open an old fracture in his skull, which had been left from a fall when he was just six years old.

John's worried workmates called an ambulance and he was rushed into hospital, where surgeons had to glue his skull back together, and then put dozens of stitches into the wound on his scalp, to hold it together.

John, whose winnings only came to a few pounds, later vowed to keep a poker face next time he played the game.

HUMILIATING HAND

MANHATTAN, 1995

Four commuters enjoying a game of poker on their Manhattan train were arrested by police and charged with possessing a 'gambling device' – to whit, a deck of cards.

When it became clear they were playing among friends the charges were dropped.

However, the four sued railway company Metro North for $4million, claiming 'undeserved public humiliation' as a result of being handcuffed and frogmarched off the train.

In May 1995 the company settled out of court for an undisclosed sum.

POKER GHOST?

Author and founder of the American Ghost Society, Troy Taylor, may well have tracked down a very rare and elusive phenomenon – the poker ghost.

In autumn 1996 Troy was called in to investigate when strange and unaccountable noises and the occasional inexplicable sighting were reported at premises that had once operated as an illegal gambling house during the days of prohibition in Decatur, Illinois.

Troy took a look around the third floor where the unaccountable events had been witnessed and 'noticed there was a sharp chill to the air – it was odd that on the third floor of an old building on a very warm afternoon it would be cooler than the lower floors'.

Troy recalled, 'I had been inside one of the rooms and had left for a few minutes. I returned a short time later and discovered two vintage playing cards had mysteriously appeared on the floor. They had not been there previously, but I still could have written the whole thing off to coincidence, if not for the fact that I discovered them in the same corner of the room where I had felt the "presence".' On an earlier visit he had felt a 'chilling, tingling sensation' only to learn that it had been the location of a man's death in the 1930s.

'It made me wonder, if a man had really been killed in that corner, just what cards had he been holding in his hand? I remain convinced that this location is truly haunted.'

189

HOLE TRUTH

1997

Harry Orenstein is one of the unsung heroes of poker, but for whom the boom in the televised version of the game would have been significantly delayed.

For in 1997 Orenstein first patented the idea for the 'hole cam', the camera used to show poker players' hole cards to TV viewers. The cam was first introduced by the Travel Channel in 2003 for its coverage of the World Poker Tour.

This was not Orenstein's first inspired idea – he is also the inventor of an all-time favourite toy for kids, Transformers.

HARD TO SWALLOW

NICE, 1998

French gambler Adrian Marque from Nice became incredibly jealous when his fellow poker player Louis Guilhot scooped a hand with three kings.

Marque 'celebrated' Guilhot's victory by stuffing poker chips down his throat and murdering him instantly.

GETTING PRIORITIES RIGHT

OREGON, 1998

The Oregon State Lottery Commission spent $90,000 obtaining expert advice on how to ensure that, should a major disaster strike the area, residents would still be able to continue playing video poker and gambling on the lottery.

Oddly enough, not everyone seemed to believe this was an appropriate or worthwhile use of funds, but a spokesman told the media in March 1998 that, as gambling was generating the equivalent of £700,000 a day in profits for the state, it made sound financial sense.

DON'T PLAY POKER IN VEGAS IN
JANUARY ON A WEDNESDAY

LAS VEGAS, 1998

After studying the details of the deaths of some four hundred poker players, dice rollers and fruit-machine merchants in Vegas in recent years, Dr Don Jason revealed in the American *Journal of Forensic Medicine and Pathology* that heart attacks were the major cause of death.

Dr Jason also discovered that January is the top month for such deaths, and that the days on which the greatest number of casino patrons are prone to play their final hand are Saturdays, Sundays and Wednesdays.

WHAT PLANET ARE THEY ON?

CYBERSPACE, 1998

Planet Poker became the first online poker site in 1998, and enjoyed solo status as the only poker room of its type for a short period before others caught on and raced to catch up. 'Suddenly, it was possible for people all over the world to hone their Texas Hold 'em skills in front of computer terminals, without feeling like they were betting the house or the children's college fund, or the safety of themselves and their loved ones,' observed *Independent* writer Andrew Gumbel.

Paradise Poker came on the scene in 1999 and rapidly became an industry leader.

In 2000 a new site called Poker Spot made a big impression – ultimately for the wrong reasons. Founded by player Dutch Boyd, it offered the first online tournaments, but became controversial when it was plagued by troubles of various types and eventually closed down.

By 2006 the value of online sites was illustrated in February when an announcement appeared in the media declaring, 'PartyGaming has agreed to pay Empire Online a cash consideration of US$250m for its white-label poker site EmpirePoker.com as part of a deal to end the legal dispute between the two companies.' But by the end of that year as US authorities made it difficult, if not impossible, for enthusiasts to play online there, many wondered if the boom might be over, and, perhaps, conditions right for a new kind of 'prohibition' to arise.

THE MODEL POKER PRO

Why would a female poker player, little known outside the game, be cited in the 2000 edition of the *Guinness Book of World Records* for being 'the most downloaded woman on the Internet in 1999'?

Well, perhaps it had something to do with the fact that, as the website pokerlistings.com revealed, 'Cindy Margolis is a former model who has been featured in a slew of publications, including numerous appearances in *Playboy*.'

Cindy is no mean poker player, though, and in 2006 was teamed up with fellow photogenic player Cyndy Violette, who boasted tournament winnings of almost $1m, in a poker reality TV series in which the pair competed heads-up against 'Average Joes' from across the USA.

Purely in the interests of research I decided to take a look at Internet coverage of Cindy, and the white-bikini-clad photograph of her gracing her newly opened website Cindyspoker.com was certainly fetching. But there was not a great deal of information about Cindy herself and her poker career to be discovered there, so I clicked on a further information button and found myself transported to Cindymargolis.com, where I was greeted by another photo of Cindy, this time in black gear. Eventually I found out some hard information on Cindy. She was born in 1965. That's it.

I suspect she will be around on the periphery of the poker scene for some time – almost certainly because of her ability to play the game, despite what critics may suggest to the contrary.

FAREWELL, THEN, LONG GONE SILVER, POKER PARROT

HOLLYWOOD PARK, USA, 2000

Given that his nicknames are 'The Mad Genius' and 'Crazy Mike', it is perhaps not that much of a surprise that when the legendary poker writer, player and thinker Mike Caro decided to set up his own Mike Caro University of Poker he should have made its official mascot an African Grey parrot called Silver.

While the university offered 'a complete free education in poker, gambling and life-strategy', the parrot became a popular figure in his own right, having a poker book dedicated to him, making an appearance in a poker video, and attending graduation ceremonies for the MCU Introduction to Poker course at Hollywood Park.

This latter event saw Silver create something of a stir when chief administrator Debbie Parks began to speak. 'Silver seemed shocked by the shattered silence,' recalled Caro, 'and shouted, "Be quiet." The room was washed in laughter. In a perverse way, this made me proud.'

Caro bought Silver for his wife Phylis on their fifth wedding anniversary in 1991. 'It was just a happy accident that I brought home an African Grey parrot and later learned about ongoing scientific studies that ranked them among the smartest non-humans on earth.'

Not quite smart enough actually to play poker, perhaps, but he certainly made an impression on those among the poker community who heard of or met him. So the Caros were devastated when, on 29 January 2000, 'although under the care of one of the best specialists in the world, Silver, who had developed an extensive vocabulary, died peacefully at the age of just twelve'.

Caro announced in 2002 that the new official mascot of the University of Poker was to be Powder, an umbrella cockatoo, born in 2000. Apparently he is 'slowly, very slowly, learning to play poker as part of his assigned duties as the new MCU mascot,' said Caro. 'We're not sure what poker terms he already knows.'

Who said poker is for the birds!

SHOW GOES ON – AFTER THE FUNERAL

CARDIFF, 2001

Hemish Shah was one of Britain's greatest poker players. But the illness that would kill him struck as he achieved his greatest performance at the poker table, then took his life as his friends battled to win a prestigious televised tournament.

Contrary to the belief of many cynics, poker players do have hearts. They called a halt to the TV tournament to attend the funeral of the 33-year-old.

Shah had developed stomach cramps during the $5,000 limit hold 'em event at the Poker World Series in Vegas during 2001. Despite the pain, which left him doubled up in his chair, he played on to win the title, $312,340 in prize money and, perhaps most importantly, his winner's bracelet.

Hemish flew back to London but his health never recovered and he died of cardiac arrest on 5 September 2001 while filming for Channel 4's *Late Night Poker* was taking place in Cardiff.

Hemish had played in an earlier series of the event, but was unable to take part in this one because of his illness, which was well known to the players, who were stunned when news of his death came through.

'You don't often see a bunch of gamblers in tears,' wrote *Observer* poker correspondent Victoria Coren. 'Not right in the middle of a big poker tournament. And not poker players whose faces are supposed to be as unreadable as an Amy Jenkins novel.'

Then they heard that the funeral had been scheduled for the last day's filming of the show. 'The hard men in the studio didn't care about losing the £1,500 they'd paid to play, or the £10,000 prize money on offer,' recalled Coren. 'They were going to London to pay their respects.'

A compromise was arranged as an early morning semi-final was played at 7 a.m. before the TV company flew the players to London by helicopter for the funeral, and then back to play the final, 'which was played silently through the night'.

HAIR-RAISING HAND

LAS VEGAS, 2001

Andy Bellin is a fine writer on poker and a pretty decent player, too.

Having been knocked out of the 2001 World Series of Poker, the New Yorker found himself involved in a Texas Hold 'em game at Binion's casino facing an older opponent of whom he had no knowledge at all, with a $1,000 pot at stake between them.

The only thing Bellin did register about his opponent was that he 'looked exactly like Uncle Fester from the Addams family'.

Fester's main eye-catching feature is, of course, an entirely bald pate.

The hand had come down to the two of them following a series of raises and reraises.

'By the last card I had exactly what I started with, a pair of jacks.'

The only card on display outranking Bellin's jacks was a queen that had arrived on the river. There seemed to be no likely flush or straight lying in wait to beat him.

Bellin had been ending each round of betting prior to the river. He had either bet or raised, with Fester calling him.

But now Fester bet the pot – $500.

Bellin needed to give serious thought to whether he was being bluffed here. As he later wrote in his book *Poker Nation*, 'I had no real thought about him before the hand other than to picture him with a light bulb in his mouth.'

200

How to discover whether he was bluffing?

He opted for an old faithful move, making as though he was going to call the bet by moving towards his stack of chips, while out of the corner of his eye clocking his opponent for any involuntary reaction, figuring that if he slumped in his chair a little it would indicate a weak hand, but that a swift move to turn his cards over would suggest Bellin was beat.

Instead, Fester sat stock still, looking at him, before reacting angrily: 'What the hell was that, you trying to steal the money, kid? What you gonna do with it anyway, buy some Rogaine?'

Bellin noted the reference to a hair restorative and wondered why a totally bald man would taunt an only slightly receding opponent in such a way. After all, 'This man was full blown, Telly Savalas bald. I'm not even sure he had eyebrows.'

Pondering deeply, Bellin finally 'saw it for the desperate insult it was, so I called'.

Finally, Fester turned over . . . pocket tens.

Bellin had scalped him good and proper.

POKER'S ROBIN HOOD

CHICAGO, 2003

Robin Hood stole from the rich to give to the poor – Barry Greenstein devotes his energies to removing cash from the clutches of top poker players in order to hand his profits to worthy charitable causes. It's the closest we are likely to see to a Robin Hood of the green baize, rather than the greensward.

Poker writer Allyn Jaffrey Shulman dubbed Greenstein 'a modern-day Robin Hood' after interviewing him in February 2004 for *Card Player Magazine*, in which article she said he had 'dreamed of becoming an eccentric philanthropist' in order to make his mother proud of him.

'Barry Greenstein distinguishes himself by donating every penny of his tournament winnings to charity – every penny. Some of the charities, like his former high school, are not even deductible, and he ends up paying taxes on these donations,' wrote Shulman.

But Greenstein does not devote every penny he makes to charity, nor does he preach when he does. When his book *Ace on the River* was published in 2005 he was asked, 'Will some of the proceeds got to charity?' but answered, 'No. I would consider this emotional blackmail. If you want to give money to charity, do it. I never tell anyone to gamble in order to help charitable causes.'

He is clear about where his charity donations are directed. 'I give money to help young children, not poker players. If someone comes to me for help I assume he is a losing player.'

He particularly supports the charity Children, Inc. (www.children-inc.org).

In March 2003 Greenstein won a $1m stud event at Larry Flynt's Hustler Casino. He gave money away to friends and family members then donated $1,000 to each of the 440 workers in Children, Inc. who were active in 21 different countries. The money went to help all sorts of situations.

Then he won $1,278,370 by finishing fifth at the fifth annual Jack Binion World Poker Open event at Gold Strike Casino in Mississippi on 29 January 2004 – he donated the lot again, half of it to Children, Inc., the rest to various other needy recipients. 'These contributions are the best things I have ever done in my life,' he said.

Greenstein believes that he became a successful player because 'I have played cards since I was a young child. I am a mathematician. I am well versed in psychology. I am very easy going, yet very competitive.'

Born on 30 December 1954, growing up in Chicago and starting out as a computer programmer, Greenstein is aware of the importance of having something to fall back on and said he would not teach his teenage son Nathaniel to play until he had completed his education. Barry became a full-time pro in 1991.

Some have called him the biggest money-winner in the history of the game, to which he responded, 'You would have to ask Chip Reese, Doyle Brunson or the IRS about that and I'm not sure if any of them could give you an accurate answer. I wouldn't be surprised to find that a big land deal was decided by a poker game or maybe a kingdom traded hands at the turn of card. The winner could declare himself to be the biggest winner in poker history.'

Barry's closest friend is Mimi Tran. When they met she was a small-time poker player. The pair struck a deal. Greenstein would teach Mimi how to improve her poker if she taught him Vietnamese. He became a basic Vietnamese speaker, she became a high-stakes player, rated one of the top ten females in the game. He claims this makes him the better teacher. She counters that she must be the better student.

In her comprehensive article about Greenstein, Shulman

seemed to capture his motivation when she concluded, 'If Barry's mother were alive to see him today, she would be so proud of her modern-day Robin Hood.'

In February 2006, Greenstein won the $100,000 prize for the 2006 WPT Invitational at the Commerce Casino in California in front of a supportive crowd chanting his name. His triumph drew a huge compliment from writer Alex Outhred: 'When you despair of all that's wrong with the world, Barry Greenstein is a shining example of what's right.'

BOOZY BILL STARTED SNOOKER'S POKER BOOM

CANADA, 2003

Bill Werbeniuk, who died in 2003, became famous as the snooker star who needed a dozen or more pints of beer to get himself in shape to play the game.

But Bill, born in Canada in January 1947, had made a living from another indoor sport before he began to crack the world's top twenty with his cue.

During his prime on the British snooker circuit he used to say that should he ever quit the game he would go back to full-time card playing. 'It's easy to bet when you've got a lot of money. I miss the challenge of living off poker when you're 3,000 miles away from home and betting all the money you have in the world. Now that's what I call real pressure.'

Bill would play poker while on the 147 circuit and recalled playing the unpredictable former snooker world champion Alex 'Hurricane' Higgins for cash, both at snooker, when the outcome would be close, and at poker, at which 'he was the worst player you could possibly imagine. It was the closest I ever got to stealing. I shudder to think how much money I took off him.'

He recalled one memorable poker hand against the Hurricane, which ended with Higgins 'jumping up and accusing me of having cards up my sleeve'.

'I said: "Higgins, I'm wearing a short-sleeved shirt".'

Bill would have been amazed at just what a hold poker has taken over many of the top players on the snooker circuit since his tragically early death at the age of 56.

One of the game's greats, Stephen Hendry, even contested the WSOP in 2005, albeit he lasted for just three hours before losing out to someone with a hand of four twos.

Confirming his enjoyment of the game, Hendry commented in October 2005, 'When you get to a snooker tournament these days, it's not a practice table the players want first, it's a poker table.'

'Poker has as tough a learning curve as snooker,' said fellow snooker world champ turned poker player Steve Davis, who should certainly know. Davis was one of the reasons his fellow snooker stars became intrigued and then almost obsessed by the game, he revealed. 'Stephen Hendry refuses to grind his way to victory: if he has a bad beat he lashes out like a wounded tiger. Mark Williams is fiercely competitive but loves bluffing.'

Jimmy White is another convert to poker, his former manager Barry Hearn recalling that, after winning a £20,000 snooker tournament prize, 'We went to a casino and after fifteen minutes Jimmy had lost £15,000. His mentality was not, "Shit, I've just lost fifteen grand", but "Hey, I'm still five grand up".'

Hearn is another fan. 'I get such a surge of adrenalin when I see really top-level poker being played.'

In 2004, snooker's reigning UK Championship title winner, Matthew Stevens, secured the biggest payday of his life – £260,000 – not by use of the cue, but by storming to victory in the 888.com Pacific Poker Open just eighteen months after first learning how to play the game.

Given all of the preceding, it was no great surprise when, in January 2006, the poker website 888.com was unveiled as the sponsor for the next five years of the World Snooker Championship in what was described as 'a multimillion-pound deal'.

FAT CHANCE AND SLIM PICKINGS

LAS VEGAS, 2003

Weighty wagers involving poker players have left some with a fat chance of winning and others bemoaning slim pickings.

In 2001 former world champion, the overweight Doyle Brunson – then tipping the scales at 398lb – took on a wager against a consortium of rival players who had offered him odds of 10–1 to his stake of $100,000 that he would be unable to shed enough weight to dip below the 300lb mark. Anxious lest Brunson might resort to desperate tactics to win the bet, it was stipulated that should he have any part of his body amputated, removed or taken out, that part must be weighed and added to his body weight.

He had two years to get rid of the excess baggage and when the first twelve months had passed and he had lost not a single pound, the warning of a poker pal – 'I've got more chance of becoming president than you have of losing that weight' – looked spot on.

The hefty stake, which resulted in potential winnings of one million dollars, then persuaded Brunson to enlist the assistance of both Weight Watchers and a certain Atkins Diet as he endeavoured to shed the pounds – eventually doing so to leave his challengers a million dollars the poorer.

Two years later, in 2005, players Mike 'The Mouth' Matusow and Erick Lindgren put up $20,000 per side to see which of them could lose the most weight in an agreed period of time.

'I dropped seventeen pounds and still lost the bet,' groaned

207

a slimmer Matusow, explaining, 'He lost an extra two pounds, but he sandbagged me. He told me he couldn't lose any more weight – he looked like a fat pig and I believed him. It was bullshit. He admitted it later.'

Back in 1969, WSOP champ-to-be Amarillo Slim teamed up with casino boss Benny Binion as the pair landed a huge bet that one person could eat a quail every single day for thirty days. No such feat of gluttony had ever been witnessed before but Slim managed to come up with a winning technique to land the six-figure stake – he hired identical twins to do it between them on alternate days!

Another grub-stake wager took place when poker pro Howard Lederer, a renowned vegetarian, was challenged by fellow player David Grey for a $10,000 stake to break his principles and eat a cheeseburger.

Lederer did it, but decided to play fair and offer Grey the opportunity to win his money back – by eating a quantity of green olives, for which he was known to have a severe aversion.

Grey immediately threw Lederer another ten grand to avoid having to swallow the olives.

DO I NOT LAAK THAT?

LOS ANGELES, 2004

'It was certainly "interesting" to see a guy hop around the table, kneel down beside the dealer to get the first peek at turn cards, and thrash about on the floor after catching a miracle ace on the river to stay alive,' declared a contributor to the unofficial World Poker Tour fan site after watching perhaps the most controversial player of today, Phil Laak's extraordinary antics, including doing press-ups, at the 2004 WPT Celebrity Invitational event, which he went on to win.

Laak, known as 'The Unabomber', apparently because of the hooded top he frequently wears while playing, often pulling the top up over his head during games, also irritated another website correspondent, 'Jasonpoker', in the event by 'doing sit-ups and dancing like a dinosaur'.

Others are uncomfortable with the player's nickname. As 'Kyseralterego', who was not alone in his sentiments, wrote on wptfan.com, 'I find the name Unibomber [sic] quite offensive. The name came from a deranged killer sending mail bombs to universities. Considering the real unibomber actually killed people by his actions it would be like someone taking on the moniker of The Osama Bin Laden of Poker.'

Other correspondents described Laak as a 'moron', an 'idiot', 'rude', 'disgusting' and an 'immature dope', although in his defence others believed he was helping to lighten up the image of the game and therefore attracting more attention and new players to it as a result.

One largely approving voice, 'Cyber_20', added a warning,

though: 'His style should not be the new trend of poker, for it will eventually take away the essence and history of the game if everyone starts acting like that . . . Have any of you laughed so much when watching poker before?'

But 'bryannyc11' shrewdly observed, 'His tactics are annoying and at times really entertaining, but poker is a psychological game and he truly understands that. His antics take the players at the table out of their routine and may hurt their concentration.'

The sunglasses-wearing Laak, who has a degree in mechanical engineering, was born in 1972 in Dublin but raised in Wellesley, Massachusetts, later relocating to California. He dated actress and fellow poker high-flyer Jennifer Tilly, who then became known as 'The Unabombshell'. In June 2005 he finished second to Johnny Chan in the $2,500 buy-in pot-limit hold 'em World Series of Poker event on the same day that his girlfriend Tilly won a WSOP bracelet, then the next month he beat the 'PokerProbot', then the best poker robot in the world.

A skilled tournament backgammon player, he had worked as an engineer, a repo man, bookie and real-estate investor before getting into poker. 'In the poker world he is both loved and scorned,' declares the website Wikipedia, adding, 'His antics at the table often ruffle a few feathers but his skill is undeniable.'

By 2005 he was estimated to have won over $500,000 from the game and had become host of the E! Entertainment television series *Hollywood Hold 'Em*.

He first began playing the game in underground clubs in New York and was then tipped off about a promising game in the San Jose area of California. There he teamed up and lived with fellow player Antonio Esfandiari; they remain friends.

Questioned on why he plays poker, Laak told a website, 'All the decisions of my life are based on satisfying three primary functions: fun, freedom and fulfilment. Poker is a blend of them all.'

HOW BEN JACKED IT IN

CALIFORNIA, 2004

Ben Affleck, the superstar actor, became the first high-profile A-list celebrity to win a major poker tournament when he landed the $356,400 first prize in the Commerce Casino California State Poker Championship on 23 June 2004.

Affleck had to see off a field of 90 players in the $10,000 buy-in event – among them another major movie name, Tobey Maguire, who went out on the first day of the three-day contest, but stayed around to watch the outcome. Affleck left poker pro Stan Goldstein in second place as he used a pair of jacks to land the spoils.

Not all of Affleck's gambling exploits have furthered his reputation, and his stormy, on-off relationship with actress Jennifer Lopez often allegedly faltered due to his love of a wager.

In August 2001 it was reported by LA showbiz reporter Gary Morgan that 'film star Ben Affleck booked himself into a clinic after winning $50,000 at a boozy all-night gambling session'. Morgan also quoted Vegas columnist Norm Clarke as saying, 'He has a $150,000 betting limit at the Hard Rock Casino, but I'm told owner Peter Morton allows him some flexibility. He is allowed to bet double the house limit of $10,000 per play.'

Affleck, who improved his technique after taking poker lessons from Southern California pro Amir Vahedi, is reportedly a generous presence at the gambling tables – once, in August 2000, tipping employees a total of $140,000 after a successful session at the Hard Rock. In 2004, writer Victoria

Coren wrote in the *Observer* of an occasion on which Affleck 'deliberately folded a winning hand for $13,000 because he felt his young opponent couldn't afford to lose'.

Writer Steve Badger believes Affleck's ability with the cards is related to his role in the movies. 'I don't think it is a coincidence that Affleck is a film-maker – writer, actor, producer – rather than just an actor. Film-makers must consider the whole of their project, not just the one aspect of the bigger picture that they are involved in.'

BEAL ME IN TO THE BIG GAME

DALLAS, 2004

You can't imagine a wealthy tennis enthusiast taking on top players like Roger Federer or Rafael Nadal for $1m a set; or a keen amateur golfer putting up a huge sum of money to play Tiger Woods or Vijay Singh in a winner-takes-all match. But when Texan billionaire banker Andy Beal decided to make an impact in the world of poker he set up a series of games against some of the very top professionals – and played them for millions of dollars.

News of the games soon spread, with stories flying around about how much Beal had won or lost against the top names he was taking on.

But Beal, like so many high-profile money men, was not overjoyed at the way he was being portrayed in the media – either by the reporters he suspected of trying to paint him as a mug player with more money than sense, or the pros who he thought might want to spin against him lest they were perceived to have been taken to the cleaners by a part-time poker player.

So Beal issued an open letter explaining his own take on the situation and directing a dramatic challenge against the leading lights of the game – effectively, put up or shut up.

Beal wrote his letter in September 2004, and sent it to Barry Shulman of *Card Player* magazine. He also copied in the likes of top pros Doyle Brunson, Chip Reese, Tod Forrest, Jennifer Harman, Phil Ivey, Johnny Chan and Howard Lederer.

I recently read a story in the *New York Daily News* that is an unfair mischaracterization of my recent poker experience in the Big Game, played at Bellagio (the Vegas casino).

No mention was made that I won more than $10m in the largest game ever played on May 12/13 2004. No mention was made of the fact that most of the above named professional players have substantial overall individual net losses after having played many hours against me. I concede that I am a net overall loser in the Bellagio games, although the extent of my losses is often exaggerated.

My interest has always been the intellectual challenge of competing with the best in games in which the amount bet is material to the people involved. I have played the best in the largest game ever played, and I won.

I challenge you to put up or shut up about your 'professional play'. Come to Dallas and play me for four hours a day and I will play until one of us runs out of money or cries uncle . . . you can bring your own independent dealers and your own cards and can play in a different location of your choice every day if you wish.

The two-day game at Bellagio in May 2004 was said to be $100,000–$200,000 limit hold 'em, and some idea of the size of Beal's games was revealed in an article in the *Daily Star* in December 2005: 'On varying occasions Beal was up $7m, down $6.3m, $8m up and down $5m thanks to a tour de force from 1992 WSOP Champ Hamid Dastmalchi. Amazingly, Beal finished this episode up $11.7m whereupon he paused for breath. On his return to Vegas two weeks later he promptly lost $6m in six hours to Todd Brunson, Doyle's poker-playing son. At this point Howard "The Professor" Lederer stepped up to the plate and promptly deprived Beal of another $9.3m in less than eight hours.'

EYE SAY, EYE SAY, CHAMP MAKES SPECTACLE OF HIMSELF

LAS VEGAS, 2004

Greg 'Fossilman' Raymer, a forty-year-old former attorney for drug company Pfizer, really eyeballed his opponents in the 2004 World Series of Poker in Las Vegas when he landed the title and a $5m payout.

And he did so while wearing one of the most bizarre accessories ever assumed by a world champion in any discipline – apart, perhaps, from TV wrestling.

For Fossilman – the nickname is courtesy of his wife's hobby of collecting fossils – eyed up his victory by wearing a pair of 3-D hologram lizard-eye spectacles, in a fetching shade of yellow.

Raymer, who gave up his job after his title triumph, explained how and when he came by his bizarre gimmick in an interview with *The Times* in March 2005:

The first time I entered the world poker tournament was in 2002. I came about eightieth. Just before, I'd taken Sophie and Cheryl (his daughter and wife respectively) to Disney World and bought these 3-D hologram lizard eyes. They were so funny I thought I'd put them on in the tournament.

Things can get tense at the table, so it's good to lighten things up sometimes. But when I put those glasses on, the guy I was playing freaked out and ended up throwing his hand away.

It made me think that there was more to them than I

215

realised, so I wore them again. Several players demanded that the directors stop me wearing them, but they were overruled and I've worn them ever since.

When he won the title he also told interviewers that he wore the special specs because he did not possess the ability to 'stare down' opponents.

This is not the only peculiarity associated with Raymer, who suffers from sleep apnoea, a condition in which the sufferer can temporarily stop breathing while slumbering. As a result 'I have a CPAP machine, which is an oxygen tank attached to a mask I wear over my nose.'

Raymer pays close attention to his opponents when at the table. 'When you're sitting round a table a player's demeanour can be the crucial tell of how he is doing.' One of his techniques is to study a player's chest in an effort to gauge whether his heart rate is increasing through nerves, thus making him breathe more quickly – a move which may not go down well with modest female players.

And now poker is in his family, with wife Cheryl deciding that if she can't beat the game she might as well join him in playing it. She has already chalked up a tournament victory – without the lizard eyes.

In December 2004 Raymer discovered life isn't all roses and wine when you are world champ. Returning to his hotel room at the Bellagio in Vegas, having won an estimated $150,000 at a cash game, he was attacked by two would-be robbers, one of whom pointed a gun at him and demanded, 'We just want the money.'

Raymer wasn't about to hand it over, so wrestled with his burly assailants, throwing one to the ground as he called for security help, which soon arrived, causing the attackers to run off without the cash.

Then in early 2006 Raymer staked a claim to an unwanted title – the pro to have travelled the furthest to get the least in the shortest time.

He flew through the night from his North Carolina home to France for the French Open event, which had attracted some

434 players. Raymer arrived just in time to take his seat. Five minutes later he was out of the tournament.

He came up against Nottingham's Julian Thew, who had been dealt two aces. Raymer was holding queen and ten of diamonds and called.

The flop showed another ten and two diamonds, leaving Raymer looking for one more diamond, or a queen or ten to have a very strong hand.

Thew bet again; Raymer raised him.

The Englishman put in a strong re-raise, and Raymer responded by going all-in.

'Neither player was willing to capitulate and considered it an early opportunity to catapult into the chip-lead,' said eye-witness writer Howard Swains.

Thew called. Raymer did not draw the diamond, queen or ten he needed and was left kicking his heels signing autographs and posing for photographs until he could return home.

POKER NETS NEW PRO

2004

Yevgeny Kafelnikov, the world number-one tennis player in 1999, French Open winner in 1996 and Aussie Open winner in 1999, stunned the sporting world when he announced in November 2004 that he was quitting the game to become a poker pro.

'In both tennis and poker you've got to go on believing in yourself until the very last moment,' declared Kafelnikov, who had, earlier in his sporting life, declared that he was about to give up tennis for golf. 'I have won tennis matches from 1–5 down in the final set, and I've won poker tournaments – small ones as yet – when I have been all-in several times before clawing back.'

'Yevgeny is a gifted poker player who is certain to do well at the highest level of the game,' predicted top player Dave Colclough.

Kafelnikov was introduced to poker by old friend Kirill Gerasimov in 2003. And he remains convinced that, just like in sport, fitness is an important attribute in poker: 'If you watch other poker players as carefully as I do, you can see the fat and out-of-condition ones losing their concentration over the long periods of time that many games take,' he told interviewer Elkan Allen in 2004. 'That doesn't happen to people who keep themselves really fit. Your brain gets fit along with your body. So it's thanks to tennis that I am winning at poker.'

In October 2004, Kafelnikov won the Korona Russian Poker

Championships in Moscow. In 2005 he almost made the final table of the stud section of the WSOP.

Perhaps Kafelnikov's enthusiasm was infecting other members of the tennis circuit, for leading player James Blake, dubbed 'an ace on the court but a wild card at the poker table', burst onto the scene in Bravo Network's *Celebrity Poker Showdown* in June 2004.

Commented Blake, 'Playing Texas Hold 'em is a lot of fun and it's really addictive.'

During Wimbledon 2006 he told of how his doubles partner Todd Martin had improved both his tennis and his poker: 'Todd preached patience all the time because I'd bail out of points too soon and go for winners. Now I watch him play poker and I tell him, "Do you realise what you're doing? You need to be patient."'

POKER GOES BARKING MAD

NEW YORK, 2005

Two paintings of dogs playing poker sold for a barking-mad price of $590,400 at an auction held at Doyle New York in February 2005.

The estimate put on the two works by Cassius Marcellus Coolidge, dating from 1903, had been between $30,000 and $50,000, but produced just under three minutes of intense bidding, forcing the price up. They were eventually purchased by a private collector from New York City who remained anonymous.

Entitled *A Bold Bluff* and *Waterloo: Two*, 'the sequential narrative follows the same "players" in the course of a hand of poker,' explained the auction-house information. 'In the first, our main character, the St Bernard, holds a weak hand as the rest of the crew maintains their best poker faces. In the following scene, we see the St Bernard raking in the large pot, much to the very obvious dismay of his fellow players.'

The sale made a world record amount for Coolidge's work. He created the oil paintings in 1903 for a Minnesota advertising company called Brown & Bigelow. There were sixteen of them in all, nine of which depicted dogs around a poker table.

The versatile Coolidge was, as well as pursuing his artistic talents, a banker, shopkeeper, inventor and painter, who also wrote an opera.

His work has even inspired a website, DogsPlayingPoker.org, which boasts that it is 'one of, if not the, biggest resource for all things with dogs playing poker'.

When the originals were sold for over half a million dollars, the website warned owners of prints of the works, 'You might be able to get $10 for it on eBay.'

The auction was not the first time these paintings had entered the public consciousness. In June 2004, the Sands Casino Hotel in Atlantic City used five real live canines to re-create one of Coolidge's doggy poker hands, and were only delayed minimally when 'Lucky Louise' got out of her seat and walked across the top of the green felt table, wagging her tail – not a problem often encountered by most dealers.

HOW MUCH TO GIVE UP SEX?

USA, 2005

Poker Stars, the online poker site, commissioned a survey to discover just how much a poker hand would have to be worth to persuade players to give up sex in return for a guaranteed win.

Research company Strategy One carried out the nationwide survey in the US that, in spring 2005, revealed that over two-thirds of American men would give up sex for a year in return for a poker win of $2.3m, while women were reportedly prepared to give up for a little less – $1.9m.

The survey also invited respondents to nominate the person they would most like to play poker with – George W Bush emerged as the top choice for men, and Oprah Winfrey for women.

SWAT'S GOING ON?

COLORADO, 2005

Twenty-two players enjoying what they thought was a quiet game of poker in a Colorado club were shocked when the place was raided by a 52-strong SWAT team on 26 April 2005.

Among the players arrested during the raid at the Guadala Jarra in Palmer Lake were Al Karn, former police chief of a neighbouring town, and Palmer Lake town council member Trish Flake. Karn and the rest were charged for 'knowingly participating in professional gambling'.

When they heard of the raid, the district attorney's office offered to dismiss charges in return for an agreement to donate $50 to a charity of each player's choice.

All but three agreed.

Trish Flake was not among them, nor was her husband Ed and local resident Diane DeKeyser. All three believed they had done nothing wrong and wanted to fight the charges in court.

Trish Lake described what had happened during the raid, saying that police had jumped out of vans and stormed the building with guns drawn, shouting, 'Put your hands up. This is a raid.'

She continued, 'It was the most frightening thing I've ever seen. We had lasers on our heads and chests. The place was surrounded. It was like Hollywood.'

In January 2006, Trish Lake and her two fellow defendants won their case. According to state law, card games can be played in businesses and liquor establishments only when the games are not considered gambling. But the law also states that gambling is legal in the state between people who have a bona fide social relationship and where all money is distributed as prizes.

BETROSEXUALS

CYBERSPACE, 2005

National tabloid newspapers got very excited about online poker 'gender-bending' in August 2005, with both the *Daily Star* and *Daily Mirror* running stories headlined 'Betrosexuals'.

The stories revealed that online players were looking to boost their chances of success by deliberately registering under names suggesting they were a different sex. 'Men are registering as women, and men as women, because they believe it fools opponents into changing their tactics on the table,' reported the *Star*.

The story emanated from a 'study' by website ultimatepoker.com, which reported that a player called 'TheDaddy10' won £2,000 in a single high-stakes game, then revealed that 'he' was a 27-year-old female secretary from Kent.

Other players trying to confuse opponents included 'Dave Mad-Dog Jones', 'Poker Boy', 'Ace-Kicker Armstrong' and 'John "The Wolf" Hearn', all of whom were women, while the most popular name for men playing as women was, imaginatively, Queen of Hearts.

One in nine men enter online tournaments disguised as women and 23 per cent of women do the opposite, claimed the survey. Analysing the research, psychologist and gambling expert Mark Griffiths of Nottingham Trent University commented, 'Reading body language and facial expressions has always been a big part of poker, now online poker rooms allow people to pull the ultimate bluff. If your opponent thinks

225

that you're the opposite sex then that can lead them to make all sorts of judgements about your character that affect how they play.'

LADY LUCK

MIDDLESEX, 2005

'Nine months ago I was playing online for fifty cents and a dollar. It's an unbelievable turnaround,' beamed Sky TV's *Soccer AM* star Helen Chamberlain after collecting a £270,000 prize in the 2005 Ladbrokes Poker Million Final.

'I love it and I hate it,' said the excited presenter, who said she would be spending the cash on paying off her mother's mortgage and buying herself a second-hand Aston Martin. 'Your insides are going all over the place. You cannot jump up and down all over the place like football.'

Helen finished runner-up in the six-player final, which took place on familiar territory – Sky's Isleworth, Middlesex studios – behind 42-year-old Romford fork-lift truck driver Tony Jones. He scooped the £560,000 top prize, despite having only started playing eighteen months earlier.

After the game, Helen commented, 'Before the final the eventual winner said that I was the opponent he feared most because he had been watching me in the heats and the semi-finals and he couldn't work out my style.

'The point was, I didn't have one.'

Helen's fascination with poker began to run out in 2006, despite the prize money she had picked up, and in May she announced she would not contest the Poker Million again. 'Sitting in silence for four or five hours round a table of people who you know are out to smash you to bits at every opportunity is not my idea of fun, plus I don't know one professional poker player who isn't a kook or a weirdo,' she raged.

BINNING WINNINGS

FRANCE, 2005

Roy 'The Boy' Brindley is a pro player who writes of his exploits on the ladbrokespoker.com site. In March 2005 he told the tale of a poker player who lost a hefty stash without even getting the chance to bet it on the outcome of a hand.

Brindley declined to identify the man, short of saying that he possesses 'the ego of an overinflated barrage balloon combined with a deeply sensitive character which is mortified by the remotest hint of humiliation'.

The player had just won $500,000 in a US tournament and was keen to find more action, so took a flight to Paris for an event about to start there. He checked in to a hotel, deciding to keep his winnings in the mini-safe in his room.

But he could fit only $460,000 into the safe, so had some forty grand left to conceal in an appropriate hiding place.

He came up with the idea of putting it all into his waste-paper basket: 'Boldly lining the bottom of the waste-paper basket with wads of notes, he then spruced it over with a mixture of tissues, chocolate-bar wrappers and a shampoo bottle.'

Off he went to play in his all-night poker tournament, happy that his cash was safe.

'Exactly what time the maid serviced the room the following morning is not entirely clear,' said Brindley. But it was clearly before he returned from the game.

The cash, along with the rest of the hotel's rubbish, was duly carried off to the local landfill site – never to be seen again.

CHRIST ALMIGHTY?

CYBERSPACE, 2005

Pokerjesusonline.com was the bizarre name of the new website that opened on 4 August 2005.

The site invited newcomers to send for 'Poker Jesus Online' car-bumper stickers and introduced itself to the world by announcing: 'Few people are aware of this, but when Jesus isn't answering prayers, performing miracles, leaping over tall buildings with a single bound, slaying dragons or fighting aliens on far off space ships, he likes to grab a cold one, kick his feet up, and play some poker. Jesus really loves his poker!'

It was, though, immediately obvious that the site was producing no ecclesiastical or biblical evidence to support this contention.

Now when Jesus first discovered Internet Texas Hold 'em, he just wasn't very good at it. He lost a lot of money real fast, for he quickly discovered that the poker games online are nothing like the home poker games he enjoys with his angel buddies. Losing all that hard-earned money made Jesus very very angry. He hated losing his bankroll almost as much as he hates Country Music, George W Bush, and France!

Luckily for us, Jesus took some time, studied poker strategy a great deal, and became a Super Poker Master. One of the best Super Poker Masters the world has ever seen! Why didn't he just cheat and simply read everyone's cards you might ask? Because that would be dishonest, and dishonesty makes Jesus sad.

Luckily for us Jesus doesn't want another person to experience the terrible pain of losing their entire bankroll just like he did. Poker Jesus is here to save your poker bankrolls with Texas Hold 'em beginners' low limit poker strategy guides, poker bankroll management tips, Hold 'em poker hands and odds charts, poker bonus codes, chip tricks and more! He's Jesus, he loves poker, and he's online!

Yes, it's a deliberately provocative marketing technique for a poker site desperately seeking to position itself as cool, trendy and cutting edge.

Equally tawdry in its unsubtle efforts to shock, around the same time bookmaker Paddy Power promoted its own poker website by taking the well-known image of Da Vinci's *Last Supper* and transforming it into a scene of Jesus and his Apostles engaged in various gambling activities.

Clearly seeking to drum up a bogus scandal, the campaign succeeded in making the company seem unsubtle, unimaginative and tacky, particularly via a quote attributed to them: 'Who said that Paddy Power were just bookies? This ad shows the great range of fun and games at paddypower.com. Jesus might have all the chips, but Judas has something up his sleeve.'

As the book went to press I was not aware of either company approaching top player Chris 'Jesus' Ferguson – so called because of his supposed physical resemblance to the Son of God – to join them.

Jesus was also the star of a set of poker chips being sold as 'Faith Chips' on the kerusso.com website in 2005, which explained, 'Because poker is so popular right now the design of the chip creates a curiosity about the message. It's really no different than using something ordinary, like a T-shirt, to share the Gospel.' The messages on the chips included: 'Jesus knew how to Hold 'em: John 10:28'; 'Accept Jesus Before You Cash In Your Chips'; 'Take The Sure Bet: Jesus'; and 'Jesus Went All In For You: John 3:16.'

WATERED-DOWN POKER CHAMP

ST KITTS, 2005

Finland's Juha Helppi won the first underwater poker tournament when he emerged from the depths of the ocean off the coast of St Kitts to claim the first InterPoker.com Extreme Poker Championship in November 2005.

Helppi had taken a deep breath as he beat off a determined but watery challenge from other contenders who were clearly out of their depth, such as pro Phil Laak and Kenna James, Internet qualifier Louise H from Denmark and InterPoker representative Peter Marcus.

Snorkelling spectators watched the action, which became a little jumpy as one hand was played out to the accompanying presence of a potentially dangerous stingray.

Beaten player Phil Laak played tribute to the winner but drew attention to the unique difficulties of this version of the game: 'I honestly thought that when his mask filled with water that I could take advantage of his broken concentration.'

'I've been present at some of the most electric moments in poker history, but this one tops them all,' said Peter Marcus, calling for Extreme Underwater Poker to be declared an Olympic sport.

The tournament undoubtedly gave a new level of meaning to 'the River'. Winner Helppi was rewarded with a Caribbean Poker Classic Extreme Poker Bracelet, made from authentic Caribbean seashells.

The table they played on was submerged using weighted anchors. Among the rules were that 'players would be disqualified if they floated away or surfaced'.

Organisers were delighted with the success of the event and promised/threatened to introduce tournaments floating on the Dead Sea, while white-water rafting, on mountaintops, on desert plains and in Arctic wastelands.

In a similar vein, as the players were knocked out of the Interpoker Extreme Challenge in Vegas in July 2006 they had to parachute out of the plane the game was taking place in. Out went Phil Laak, Jamie Glasser, Fraser Linkleter and Patrick Neary. Laak commented, 'The pressure was unbelievable, knowing that if someone called my bluff I would have to jump out of a plane.'

The contest was won by 29-year-old New York pro Nick 'Stoxtrader' Grudzien. Having won, Grudzien came down in the plane – only to go back up for a jump.

OLD TIMERS

SCOTLAND, 2005

Gala Maybury casino in Scotland claimed a new world record for the oldest heads-up match ever when, during 2005, 84-year-old Emma Dray defeated 87-year-old Reg Poolman to win their 41-runner no-limit hold 'em tournament first prize of £1,330.

CHARGED PLAYERS DEALT WRONG HAND

BALTIMORE, 2005

Prosecutors had to drop charges against eighty poker players who they arrested during a raid in November 2005 on Baltimore's Owl's Nest poker club. They seized $25,000 in cash in the city's biggest gambling raid since the unlamented days of Prohibition.

Those arrested were threatened with up to a year in jail, but the charges laid were under a section of the law concerning a person 'keeping, renting, using or occupying' a building for the purpose of gambling.

But the police were devastated to discover that they should have used an entirely different subsection – one that prohibits a 'bet, wager or gamble' – against the players.

As a result the Baltimore Eighty went free without a stain on their character.

PLAYING TO THE DEATH

MEXICO, 2005

An evening poker game ended in mass slaughter in 2005 as gunmen opened fire on the game, killing five players.

The game was taking place in the Mexican border city of Nuevo Laredo in December 2005 at around 9 p.m. in a mechanic's garage when the shoot-out began.

Police, who said the poker players met regularly at the venue, revealed that one of the victims was a former police officer who sold cars for a living, and blamed 'the city's ongoing struggle with violence on warring drug cartels' – the incident took to 175 the number of criminal 'executions' in Nuevo Laredo during 2005.

KNOCKOUT PRIZE

LAS VEGAS, 2005

Mike Tyson's former residence, a house in Vegas worth $4m, was named as the first prize in a multimillion-dollar poker tournament being set up by English millionaire Dominic Marrocco, the owner of the property, in December 2005.

Marrocco was planning to make the house the main prize for a reality TV show that would involve hundreds of poker players competing against each other.

'If the series goes through,' reported Lianne Elias, 'four players will advance from the vast playing field to take their seats alongside Marrocco and Tyson at a final table located on the basketball court in the grounds of the mansion.'

Marrocco explained, 'People might think I'm some kind of crazy English eccentric giving away Tyson's house, but contestants pay thousands of dollars each to enter high-stakes poker tournaments, plus there are the rights to the reality TV show. I have the chance to keep the house if I win the tournament but, if I don't, I will walk to my house next door, shut the door behind me and have still made money. I think Mike would appreciate the chance to take part and win back his home – as long as he doesn't bite anyone's ears!'

WE WISH YOU A POKER CHRISTMAS

UK, 2005

Poker paraphernalia set new records as Christmas present material during the 2005 festive period.

'More than a million poker games and products were sold before December 25,' reported *The Times* of the British market, adding, 'One producer alone made more than a million poker sets for sale to department stores and toy shops in 2005, nearly double that of the year before.'

Even the world famous Hamleys toy store was selling poker equipment. 'This was a major trend this Christmas. We brought in new ranges this year to cater for demand.'

Debenhams was so impressed with the purchase power of poker they vowed to keep such products in their stores at least until the next Father's Day. John Lewis said that poker sales had doubled year on year.

And Amazon, the online store, was even selling a circular poker table-top with built-in drinks holders.

It wasn't only a British phenomenon, though, with the Swedes also catching on to the poker craze. The Swedish Research Institute of Trade reported that for Swedes, 'the gift of the moment is a poker set'. Svenska Spel, the state gambling monopoly, revealed that there are 200,000 Internet poker players in the country. And American poker fans were offered the opportunity of purchasing 'Monty Python Poker Gift Sets' among other poker novelties.

Re: Creation, a company making many poker products, said that for the first time in 2005 it had produced over one million poker sets, up from 600,000 the year before.

And the website poker-wear.com was offering a plethora of items like poker tables, jerseys (male and female), hats, jewellery, art prints, posters, signs, watches, gift baskets, and collectables like 'pokerheads', which are seven-inch figurines created from polyresin material and modelled in the likeness of top players like Doyle Brunson, Phil Hellmuth, etc.

MIND YOUR LANGUAGE

2005

In his first tournament after winning the 2005 WSOP, Joseph Hachem finished out of the prize money.

The tournament featured a controversial 'F-Bomb' rule – anyone caught using the swear word beginning with that letter was 'fined' by a ten-minute penalty away from the table. Some were delighted – female pro Lucy Rokach approved and called for further measures: 'All naughty players should be banished, preferably wearing a dunce's cap with a F emblazoned on it.'

But Keith 'The Camel' Hawkins was outraged. 'If someone swears to himself or uses a swear word in conversation, penalising him is ridiculous. We are not playing in a kindergarten. We are adults playing in a casino. Treat us with a bit of respect, please.'

One player, Rafi Amit, was penalised when he was reported by another player. He received the ten-minute penalty and was blinded off at a rate of $16,000 per hand.

No one apparently asked Mike 'The Mouth' Matusow for his opinion after he picked up no fewer than five F-Bomb penalties.

FELINE GOOD

MARYLAND, 2005

Bruce Bartfeld credited his success in an online poker tournament in December 2005 to his cat, Sadie.

The 52-year-old pet-store owner from Churchville, Maryland won a Ferrari F430 Coupe in a tournament hosted by PartyPoker.net and explained, 'I was really short-stacked. Then Sadie decided to jump up and sit on my lap and my luck changed for the better. They say cats have nine lives, Sadie certainly gave me a lifeline.'

Bartfeld was also purring with pleasure, as his prize also included taking part in the PartyPoker.com Million V Cruise around the Cayman Islands, giving him the chance to compete for the $5m prize pool – but without Sadie.

225,000 (PARTLY) NAKED POKER PLAYERS

ONLINE, 2005

At any one time, 225,000 online gamblers could be playing poker and other casino games in a state of undress, according to a survey on online poker and casino players carried out in November and December of 2005.

That's if you can accept the reckoning that goes to make up this somewhat startling figure. The survey was carried out among 342 UK-based readers of *Online Gambler Magazine*, of whom 15 per cent – or about fifty individuals – revealed 'that they play online in their underwear or completely in the nude'.

What also emerged from this survey was that 'nearly one tenth of those online poker and casino players surveyed confirmed that they would consider giving up their jobs to play online professionally'.

I can't help thinking that the word 'consider' may be significant here.

Three per cent of those questioned admitted to playing online during office hours, with 60 per cent clocking up over five hours a week, and a quarter – 'equating to approximately 375,000 UK online poker and casino players' – playing for over ten hours a week.

Poker emerged as clearly the most popular online betting activity, with Texas Hold 'em leading the way, followed by blackjack, roulette, and then other forms of poker.

Around 38 per cent said they gave up watching TV to play online, while 19 per cent forfeited a drink in the pub. More

241

interesting, perhaps, is the revelation that 8 per cent 'sacrifice time with their partner' to play poker, and 5 per cent forgo sex.

Over half of the respondents spent £50 or less per month on their gambling, of which 38 per cent spent under £20 – so I presume we are safe in thinking that Messrs Brunson and Hellmuth didn't take part in the survey.

POKER USED TO FIGHT BIRD FLU!

CHINA, 2005

Chinese health authorities in the country's northern Shanxi province were using poker's popularity to spread information about how to combat the potentially deadly bird flu, it was revealed in December 2005.

The information was printed on playing cards specially created and then distributed to the poker-crazy inhabitants of the area. The pack was developed by a hospital in Yuncheng City and each card contained information on the disease, how it is transmitted, and what effect it has on humans and livestock.

'It is hoped the playing cards will help popularise knowledge of the disease among people as they go about participating in their regular poker games,' said a statement.

IS CASTRO A POKER ACE?

CYBERSPACE, 2006

A poker website carried out a survey asking respondents to decide who would win a mythical poker game between George W Bush, Tony Blair, Fidel Castro, Kim Jong II and Saddam Hussein.

The majority verdict was that the Cuban ace, Castro, would emerge victorious.

Another question asked by the Paddy Power report: 'Poker 2006: The State of Play' produced the startling statistic that over 50% of all poker players surveyed 'have played the game naked or in their underwear'.

And also that 10 per cent of players surveyed have injured themselves whilst playing poker.

ROBOT THREAT TO ONLINE POKER

CYBERSPACE, 2006

'If these programs evolve as fast as the experts predict, online poker is nothing more than a busted flush,' warned writer Phil Robinson as he drew attention to the use of 'poker robots' in online poker games.

These 'bots' have been programmed to take part in online games in which opponents will be unaware that they are taking on a machine rather than a human. And as the bot is capable of making millions of almost instant calculations designed to quantify the likelihood that it holds a winning or losing hand and bet accordingly, it is as certain as Vegas is vulgar that over any period of time it will come out on top.

A software expert, known to Robinson as 'Chopper', was in no doubt that 'there is no such thing as a fair game of online poker. It just doesn't exist. The game is completely corrupt; it has zero integrity.'

Revealing the threat to the integrity of the online game in the *Mail on Sunday*'s 'Night & Day Live' magazine, Robinson watched a bot in action in his office: 'No fireworks, no razzmatazz; just the quiet, steady accumulation of cash. The program made £40 over the course of our office day.'

Obviously forty quid is not about to bankrupt or scandalise a whole industry, but you can multiply that by vast amounts to take account of the number of bots being used and their ever-increasing efficiency as the technology and programming becomes more reliable and competent.

A man called Ray Bornert II created a bot called

245

WinHoldEm, selling for just over a hundred pounds. Pointing out that an online poker player might take up to one minute to decide what play to make, Bonert said, 'Think of what a computer can achieve in five seconds, let alone a minute.' But he acknowledges that the success of his bot could ultimately be self-defeating: 'People want to play against humans that have weaknesses, not robots. They won't stand for it.'

Already the big online poker sites are aware of the danger to their business, with Party Poker's director of corporate communications John Shepherd admitting, 'We have caught individual cheats and also groups of people who were colluding or using bots. In all cases we closed their accounts and seized their funds and barred them from our system.'

Respected professional player and poker writer David Sklansky has warned that 'the biggest problem for card rooms is the bots that are programmed to collude . . . they will be able to play an improved strategy based on knowing each other's own cards and will really cause the other players to struggle.' Sklansky believes that in a game involving three World Champion human players and three lesser players, or bots, who were able to collude, 'then all three world champions would eventually lose'.

Having investigated the threat to online poker from the march of the bots, Phil Robinson had a pessimistic take on the future: 'The online game is dead: by its very nature it is wide open to cheats and colluders.'

Infamous casino cheat Richard Marcus, who allegedly made $25m from his activities, also went public with concerns about online poker in November 2005, predicting, 'Within a short amount of time we are going to see about one in a hundred people playing honestly. The rest will be using bots, or it will be computers playing against computers.'

In 2005, 'Poker Probot', programmed by 37-year-old Hilton Givens, won the $100,000 World Series of Poker Robots tournament held at Binion's casino in Las Vegas.

After winning the event, sponsored by GoldenPalace.com, Poker Probot took on human pro Phil 'The Unabomber' Laak, in a man-versus-machine showdown, which the human won in a 399-hand shoot-out.

London pro Joe Beever has no fear of the march of the poker bot, declaring aggressively, 'Find me a poker bot and I'll play it for any amount. When it comes to poker, so much of it is human emotion, human psychology, human feeling. A computer can pick out patterns but it's very hard for a computer to understand a human poker player.'

Pro player Carl Sampson is also highly sceptical about bots. 'They don't work,' he declared in the May 2006 edition of the *WPT* magazine. 'The people selling them are con merchants, as most – if not all – sites have sniffer programs that can detect if you're running a bot on your computer. The security of top poker sites is akin to large financial institutions.' And Sampson also believes, 'There is no piece of software that can play at a pro level.'

In mid-2006 another potential threat emerged when, as magazine *Poker Europa* reported, 'A piece of software from www.cardswapelite.com is being circulated on the Internet making claims that it can change the hole cards on Party Poker and give you pocket aces every hand.'

But Partypoker.com's Warren Lush swatted the allegation. 'The software belongs in the world of computer-generated optical illusions. We have tested it and it does not work. It will only make money for the seller.'

Asked whether he believed that poker robots posed a threat to human players, former world champ Chris Moneymaker answered, 'In limit games potentially, but not in no-limit.'

Marbella Slim, the *Daily Star* newspaper's poker columnist, entered the debate in July 2006, asking, 'Why would a mega-billion-dollar business cheat when it makes totally legal fortunes by raking hundreds of games of poker a minute? Play happily in the knowledge that you are in far greater danger from a dodgy dealer in a bricks and mortar poker room than you'll ever be online.'

HOW CARL BET HIS FINGER ON A HAND

THE MIDWEST, USA, 2006

Carl Valentine announced that he had staked his right index finger on a hand of poker in possibly the most bizarre wager of its kind.

The machine-shop labourer from the Midwest was provoked into the bet following a visit from a childhood friend made good, who had become a multimillionaire via Internet marketing.

The pair got to talking about the Internet and the friend offered to bet Carl $1m that he would be unable to direct two million unique visitors to an individual website by 18 April 2006 – the friend's birthday.

Knowing full well that his labourer pal did not have that kind of money, the friend may have been a little shocked to have his bluff called when Valentine announced that he would accept the bet – and put up his right index finger as his stake. The destination of the stakes would then be decided by a heads-up poker game between the pair at the PokerRoom.com site on 18 April.

Now, cynics may suspect that this entire story was a handy publicity stunt for an Internet poker site, but on 12 December 2005, Carl's supposed website, Savemyfinger.com, duly appeared online and began to attract hits.

On the site Carl mused, 'Am I kidding? No . . . Am I nervous, Hell, yes. This is seriously not a joke.'

There is, though, a get-out for Carl. 'I told him [the friend]

248

I would bet my finger against his money. If I send two million visitors to the site I will be playing to win $1m, if not I am playing to keep my index finger.'

Valentine told pokerlistings.com, 'Obviously I am a bit crazy for accepting the proposition, but it's just a finger – I have plenty more. Besides, this is the only opportunity I will probably ever have to win $1m.'

However, as Carl's story spread around the web and the world, fingers were pointed accusingly by some digital doubters, alleging that the yarn should not be so handily accepted by site users. As the hits mounted, passing 1.5 million, Valentine's conscience was pricked, and he confessed: 'I don't think it is a big surprise to most that this, of course, was just a funny story.' Declaring that the intention of the site had been to engage in an experiment with viral marketing, he knuckled down and made a decent fist of calming detractors: 'If you were offended, I apologise.' Still, you have to hand it to him!

PAIRING UP TO GO ALL IN

LAS VEGAS, 2006

Jackie Johnson jumped in to support Gary Suffir when she saw him being criticised after losing a hand during the online tournament they were both playing in September 2004. And on 7 March 2006, at the Paris Hotel in Las Vegas, the pair were wed.

Gary, a New York attorney, and 27-year-old artist Jackie, from Vegas, were both playing in an Omaha tournament online at PartyPoker.com when 'Gary made what I considered to be a good play, but got routed by a bad beat on the river. The guy who won the hand started trashing Gary. I supported Gary in the argument and the rest, as they say, is history.' Well, once Gary had established that she was female, that is!

Inevitably the pair's honeymoon was also poker-related – taking part in the PartyPoker.com Million Cruise around the Cayman Islands and Jamaica.

Poker professionals often have a lonely life on the road, so when they do decide the time is right to team up with a member of the opposite sex it would make sense to find someone who understands the stresses and strains of their way of life.

And the number of poker pros pairing up with each other has really begun to rise. In early 2006, Steve Lipscomb, CEO and founder of the WPT, pointed out that there were no fewer than six prominent pairings of poker pros on their circuit, and observed, 'Poker couples in the WPT are like suited connectors – sequentially numbered cards of the same suit. Different in many ways they are strengthened by their likenesses.'

The happy half-dozen like-minded couples were former dealers Michael 'The Grinder' Mizrachi and Aidiliy Elviro; Jennifer Harman and Marco Traniello; Karina and Chip Jett, who both also teach the game; Marsha Waggoner and Kenna James; Juan Carlos Mortensen and Cecelia Reyes; and Phil Laak and Jennifer Tilly.

The Mizrachi–Elviro pairing even expanded itself by buying a luxurious touring bus, after a tournament win, to take them around – with the baby, Paul William, and granny in tow.

PRIESTLY POKER

ROMANIA, 2006

Vasile Mihails, parish priest for the village of Negoesti in Gorj, Romania, was fined and threatened with defrocking after he was caught playing poker in the local pub in February 2006.

The forty-year-old and two of his fellow players were fined the equivalent of £200 each for gambling illegally in an unauthorised place. A police spokesman commented to local paper *Gazeta de Sud*, 'There were nine men at the table playing poker, but only three of them had money in front of their seats. I was stoned [sic] when I heard one of them was a priest.'

Church officials said they had begun an investigation and warned that Mihails could be defrocked for 'activities incompatible with the service of a clergyman'.

The reaction to this incident was somewhat in contrast to the activities of a Canadian pastor John Van Sloten, a Calgary preacher, who in late January 2006 delivered a sermon to his 300-strong congregation at New Hope Christian Reformed Church, promoting the virtues of poker.

'In my view poker has a lot to teach us about ourselves and even God,' declared Van Sloten. Before making the sermon he said, 'I hope to talk about how God made us for gambling, how every human is made for the adrenalised-risk buzz of the game and how this is what a real and alive faith should feel like.'

Van Sloten admitted to participating in a few hands of Texas Hold 'em himself with friends, but said he is not blind to the potential perils of addiction and compulsion. 'We won't go soft on those things, because the last thing I want is the church promoting poker and half the congregation falling into gambling debt.'

Rabbi Steve Kaufman is a professor at Hebrew Union College, educated at the Jewish Theological Seminary, whose specialities include Ancient Semitic languages and academic computing. And poker – which he takes very seriously.

He has finished in the money in 25 major tournaments, making the final table of the 2000 WSOP, and plays regularly online and in Vegas, taking part in cash games at the Bellagio, among other events.

STRAIGHT UP

CYBERSPACE, 2006

ComeOutPoker.com, described as 'the world's first online poker site catering exclusively to the Gay Lesbian Bisexual Transgender (GLBT) community', launched in September 2006.

The site boasts 'the first ever gay poker game', known as ComeOut Hold 'em – in which 'all straights are eliminated' from the ranking of the hands.

DEALERS' CHOICE

MIAMI, 2006

Anthony Holden, famous for his *Big Deal* book about poker, recounted an interesting dealer incident while competing in the Ladbrokes Poker Cruise, which sailed out of Miami in mid-January 2006. 'Amid heavy weather and choppy seas, Night One turned out to be "Vomitgate" as dealers in the late-night super-satellite for tomorrow's Main Event drop as fast as the players. One dealer invents a new poker term – the "all-out" move – by throwing up on the player in seat one.'

Triple world champion Stu Ungar had his share of run-ins with dealers. A female dealer named Darlene at the Dunes casino once threatened to take him outside and beat him up.

Then, just before he was due to defend his world title in 1981, he was barred from the Horseshoe, where it was to be held, for allegedly spitting at a dealer called Franks. Only high-level diplomacy allowed the champ back in at the last minute.

Few players seem to spare much time or thought for dealers – but top female player Isabelle Mercier has a pet hate: 'Speaking in a bad manner at the dealer is totally unacceptable, but I still see it happening all the time.'

And in April 2006, Dave 'The Devilfish' Ulliott was yellow-carded while captaining England in the televised PartyPoker.com Football and Poker Legends Cup when, according to PartyPoker's Warren Lush, 'He was talking to the dealer and said she looked like a storm trooper.'

Dealers are often the butt of players' frustrations, but pro player Ashley Alterman leaped to their defence. 'Playing live,

255

you have an obligation to protect your hand yourself and to keep up with the action. If you fail to do either, and the dealer makes an error, you are the one who suffers the consequences. If you want to blame someone else when things go wrong, take up bridge.'

During the 2005 Monte Carlo Millions tournament, for which there was a $14,000 buy-in, a dealer error turned what should have been a hand-winning pair of kings for John Juanda into a flush for his opponent. Juanda, though, acknowledged defeat before shaking hands with the other players and the dealer and merely commenting, 'These things happen', to the mortified but relieved dealer.

SHADY GOINGS-ON

BOLTON, 2006

Sunglasses are often worn by 'cool' players to prevent others looking into their eyes, but they can have their drawbacks, as player Lee Wood from Bolton told the *WPT Magazine* in March 2006.

'This guy came who fancied himself as a pro. He put on silly ski-shades. Only after a few hours did we tell him we could see his cards in their reflection.'

And Phil Ivey used to be a sunglasses man, until they caused him to misread and lose a $100,000 hand, whereupon he dumped the $1,000 shades in the bin, and never again wore such specs during play.